SURE-TO-WIN
Science Fair Projects

SURE-TO-WIN
Science Fair Projects

Joe Rhatigan with Heather Smith

LARK
BOOKS

A Division of
Sterling Publishing Co., Inc.
New York

Library of Congress Cataloging-in-Publication Data

Rhatigan, Joe.
    Sure-to-win science fair projects/Joe Rhatigan with Heather Smith.
        p. cm.
    Includes index.
    ISBN 1-57990-374-6
      1. Science projects—Juvenile literature. [1. Science projects.
2. Science—Experiments. 3. Experiments] I. Smith, Heather,1974- II. Title.

    Q182.3 .R53 2001
    507'.8—dc21

                    2001016505

10 9 8 7 6 5 4 3 2

Published by Lark Books, a division of Sterling Publishing Co., Inc.
387 Park Avenue South, New York, N.Y. 10016

© 2001, Lark Books

Distributed in Canada by Sterling Publishing,
c/o Canadian Manda Group, One Atlantic Ave., Suite 105
Toronto, Ontario, Canada M6K 3E7

Distributed in the U.K. by:
Guild of Master Craftsman Publications Ltd.
Castle Place, 166 High Street, Lewes East Sussex, England BN7 1XU
Tel: (+ 44) 1273 477374, Fax: (+ 44) 1273 478606,
Email: pubs@thegmcgroup.com, Web: www.gmcpublications.com

Distributed in Australia by Capricorn Link (Australia) Pty Ltd., P.O. Box
704, Windsor, NSW 2756 Australia

If you have questions or comments about this book, please contact:
Lark Books
67 Broadway
Asheville, NC 28801
(828) 253-0467
Printed in China

ISBN 1-57990-374-6

Consultant and contributor:
Hope Pendergrass

Art director:
Thom Gaines

Design layout and production:
Theresa Gwynn

Cover design:
Kathy Holmes

Photography:
**Evan Bracken and
Richard Hasselberg**

Illustrations:
Orrin Lundgren

Editorial assistance:
Rain Newcomb

Editorial interns:
**Murphy Townsend
and Roper Cleland**

Table of Contents

Scientist or madman? You decide.

Introduction

"Huh?"
That's the sound of a scientist.
That's right, "huh."
"Hmmm."
Yep, also a scientist.
"Huh? Hmmm. Achoo!"
That's a scientist with a cold.

What do you think of when someone says "scientist"? Do you get a visual image of a man (why is it always a man?!) in a white **lab coat**, face dwarfed by his thick-lensed glasses and a disheveled mop of hair that looks like it hasn't been combed since elementary school? Well, that's certainly one way to think of a scientist. And sure, science is the stuff you learn in school. But once you've figured out that science is so much more than memorizing names and parts of stuff, you'll also realize that all you really need to be a scientist is your own **curiosity.** Now, if you look out your window and see clouds and think "where did those clouds come from?" and then sit down and watch TV for five hours, well then, you're a **couch potato,** not a scientist. But what if you decided to ask your mom where clouds came from? That's a start. Or even better (no offense intended, Mom!), you check the Internet or stick your nose in an encyclopedia. That's where science begins: you become curious about something and then seek to **answer the question** or questions you have. We all start out life being curious. Some of us have forgotten how, but all it truly takes is getting in touch with those five senses of yours.

Smell the world, look at the world (really look at it!), taste the world...okay you get the drift. Life is chock full of lots of overwhelming things we don't yet understand, but at its simplest and purest, science is the world of "huh" and "hmmm." Throw in a little **"how interesting..."** and that's all you need to get started.

This book was written primarily to help you get your "huh" and "hmmm" working again, especially if you happen to have **A SCIENCE FAIR PROJECT DEADLINE** looming. Science fairs can be a lot of fun, though sometimes they produce dread, hopelessness, and fear. No matter how you feel about your science fair project, this book can help you out.

Not only will this book help you tap your natural curiosity, but it also takes the time to break down the whole science fair experience into **small steps** that are easily understood—and that can go a long way to helping you feel eager and excited about your science fair project. There are also lots of tips, checklists, advice, and examples included, written just for you (not for your parents or teachers). Then, to top it all off, there are 51 projects **(real live projects!),** many straight from real live science fairs, that you can use for inspiration or to get you started on your own project. The projects are even set up so that if you used one of them, you wouldn't be cheating, because it would still be up to you to do the work and figure out the results.
Ready? Let's "huh" and "hmmm."

Science Fair Basics

So, what is a science fair, anyway?

Good question! So glad you asked.

Every year, thousands of students around the world are invited to participate in their school's annual science fair. Students then embark on a lengthy, often rewarding and fun, journey into the very heart of science exploration and experimentation. It's a time when students not only learn about science, but actually DO science. And teachers LOVE when that happens; you probably will as well. For example, if you're interested in tennis, you don't just read books about tennis— you play tennis. Working on a science fair project allows you to play with science and then show off your work.

Most science fairs ask their participants to research an interesting question, form an opinion as to its answer, and then devise an experiment to either prove or disprove the answer. This process is known as the *scientific method*. After all that, the students present their findings at the science fair, which is a party thrown to celebrate the students' hard work. Sometimes the presentations are judged, prizes may be awarded, and award winners may be invited to higher competitions.

Unfortunately, if you ask an older brother, sister, or friend what a science fair is, they may tell you something completely different. They might say science fairs are boring and tedious. Maybe they'll tell you the story of how they stayed up until 3 a.m. the night before the project was due. Or they may boast about having simply copied their project straight from a book or from someone else's work. If you wait until the last minute to do your project, or if you use someone else's, you, too, will find your science fair boring and tedious. But, if you're just a tad bit interested in the world around you, and you take your time with your project, and put a lot of effort into doing your own work, the science fair will feel like a celebration. And you'll probably feel pretty good about yourself and your experience, even if you don't end up winning any awards.

Whoa, back up! What's this scientific method thing?

Another wonderful question!

The bread and butter of most science fairs is the scientific method. Scientists spend a lot of time observing, experimenting, guessing, and creatively finding answers to the world's mysteries, and the scientific method is one way scientists look for answers. In a nutshell, the scientific method is a step-by-step process that helps you form a question in such a way that it can be answered, and then helps you find the answer. Here are the steps:

1. State the Question

You can't answer a question or solve a problem until you understand what you're asking. If you see a red leaf on the ground and are interested in why it's on the ground and not on the tree, you need to form a question before you can move on. You might ask, "Why do leaves turn different colors in autumn?" Now you have a definite question to answer or problem to solve.

2. Gather Background Information

This is another way of saying "do research." If you're interested in your topic, the research will be fun. What do you already know about the subject? Talk to experts. Check resources such as books and the Internet.

3. Form a Hypothesis

This is your personal opinion of what you think the answer to the question will be. It's not a wild guess, especially since you've researched the problem already, but, instead, more of an educated guess.

4. Test Your Hypothesis

This is where you get to perform an experiment to gather data, which then helps determine whether or not your hypothesis solves the problem.

5. Draw Conclusions

After examining your data from the experiment, you can draw a conclusion. Did your hypothesis hold up after analyzing your data? What happened?

Scientists developed the scientific method so that when a question forms in a scientist's mind, or when they see something curious, they can come up with a possible solution to the question and test their solution. Scientists do things this way so that if anyone else wants to find out if they're telling the truth, they can, by repeating the experiment. That's not only a courteous thing to do—it's the only way scientists will believe other scientists. If they can't see it for themselves, they will ignore you, or even worse, get angry.

Now, the scientific method can't answer every question in the universe. Astronomers, for example, can't visit distant stars and perform experiments. They rely on other techniques to find answers. But the scientific method does provide a wonderful introduction to how a lot of scientists think and work. It's a way of learning about the world, and *it's something you already know how to do.* Skeptical? Good, you've got a scientist's mind already. Here's an example:

You're hanging out at your favorite candy store, and you notice a new bubble gum that promises "THE BIGGEST AND THE BADDEST BUBBLES EVER!" You say to yourself, "Yeah right! I don't believe that for a second." But maybe, just maybe, a question pops into your head: "How do the bubbles made with this new gum compare with the bubbles made with my favorite bubble gum?" You've just stated a *problem.* Maybe, just maybe, you then ask the store owner if he or she knows if the new gum does

indeed deliver bigger and badder bubbles. You've just done some *research*. Then you purchase the new gum, along with a pack of your favorite gum, and do a simple *experiment*. You blow several bubbles with your old favorite gum. Then you blow several bubbles with the new gum. You compare the sizes of the bubbles and reach a *conclusion*.

That was easy, and you didn't even need a textbook. So, if you've ever done anything like this before, you already have the mind of a scientist, even if you don't have one of those really cool lab coats. And if you feel you don't have the mind of a scientist, don't worry, I've got one in my top desk drawer. But seriously folks...keep reading, and you too will soon wish you had a really cool lab coat.

Okay, okay, I get it. What do I do next?

Hold your horses. I'm getting to that!

The rest of this chapter will take you through each step of getting your science fair project started and

> "There's a scientist inside each one of us. Don't worry, she may tickle a little, but she's harmless." —Anonymous

finished on time, including keeping a project notebook, developing a schedule so you don't wake up the morning of the science fair panic-stricken, choosing a topic, presenting the problem, researching your topic, developing a hypothesis and a valid experiment, conducting the experiment, recording data, reaching a conclusion, writing your report, getting your display ready for the fair, and preparing for the judging. Whew!

Now, before you start hyperventilating, each of these steps will be carefully explained and broken down into easy segments. Plus, there will also be lots of examples to help explain each step, and checklists to make sure you've done everything you're supposed to do. So, take a deep breath and let's get going. Whether you're a dive-in-headfirst kind of person or a dip-in-your-big-toe-to-see-if-the-water's-too-cold person, it's time to make a splash.

DEVELOPING A PLAN OF ACTION

Every good project begins with a well-thought-out plan. Just as a movie director doesn't start filming the day she gets a new movie, you'll need to do some behind-the-scenes work on your science fair project before getting to the actual experiment. A good plan will make your life a lot easier later on down the road.

1. Buy a Notebook

You'll need a sturdy notebook that won't fall apart anytime soon, because it'll serve as your science project resource center. It's where you'll keep all your notes, thoughts, and ideas. When you're looking for an idea for a project, use the notebook to make lists of possible topics. Narrow down your topic in your notebook. Record in your notebook the titles and authors of all the books and articles you've read while doing your project research. Also, include a summary of the books and articles so you don't forget what they were about. Use your notebook to devise your experiment, record your data and observations, and draw diagrams and graphs. In other words, your notebook will provide an accurate account of your project from beginning to end and, in the process, keep you organized. Try to keep your notebook as neat as possible, but remember, this notebook is for you, not for the judges. Teachers and judges will look at your notebook to see if you've really done the work you said you did. They'll check your data and maybe get a glimpse of how you came up with your conclusion, but you won't be penalized for not having a super neat and tidy notebook.

2. Assess Your Feelings

It's not a bad idea to figure out how you feel as you embark on this big project. Are you confused, anxious, excited, bored...? Try to figure out why you feel the way you do. What's making you confused? Write down questions in your notebook, and ask your teacher or parents to help. There's an old saying that states the only dumb question is the one that's never asked. So, go ahead and ask. What's making you anxious? Do you feel you can't do a whole project? Talk to your parents or someone else you trust. Or keep reading this book. Working through your feelings about participating in a science fair is one way of making it a more rewarding experience.

3. Make a Schedule

One of the best ways to stay on top of the project and not end up a wreck the day the experiment is due is to create a schedule. A science fair project takes a lot of time and effort, but if you spread the project out over a long period of time, then you'll still have time for sports, hobbies, breathing, eating, etc. First, figure out how much time you have to complete the project, and then give yourself time to finish the whole project. There's an eight-week project schedule on page 12. Use it, or develop your own with

the help of your teacher or parents.

4. Choose a Topic

"Aaargh! I have no idea in this whole wide world what to do this science fair project on!" This is a real fear for many science fair participants. Some even say it's the hardest part of the whole project! But there are a ton of ways to find a project that you'll be interested in doing, and that's the most important thing in the whole wide world to remember: CHOOSE A PROJECT THAT'S INTERESTING TO YOU. Don't feel you have to choose something "scientific" that will please teachers, parents, or judges. You're the one who's going to be working on the project, so you should, at the very least, like the topic A LOT. Also, once you realize that you don't have to clone your cat or build a nuclear space station to do well, and that it's perfectly okay (in fact, it's preferable) to work on something that actually interests you, well, then you're halfway there. Here are some ways to help you choose a topic:

● If something hasn't already popped into your mind, ask yourself these questions:

▶ What interests me?

▶ What do I like to do?

▶ Is there something I've always wanted to know the answer to?

Make a list of your responses to one or more of these questions in your notebook.

● Look closely at the world around you. Do what you usually do, but pay closer attention to your surroundings. If you watch television, listen closely to the commercials. Are they telling the truth? Or, if you take a bus home from school every day, think about the bus. Is there a more environmentally friendly way to power the bus? Think about where your garbage goes. Wonder about how the things you take for granted work, such as microwave ovens, remote controls,

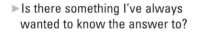

and fax machines. We have become so accustomed to technology that we forget to wonder how things work. Write your observations down in your notebook, and see if any of them spark an interest.

● Explore what your parents, family members, and neighbors do for a living. If their jobs intrigue you, ask questions about what they do, and look for possible topics. Say you have a neighbor who practices holistic medicine. You could ask her what holistic medicine is and how it differs from traditional medicine. Then, BOOM, there's your topic.

● Look at science fair books (though of course, this one's the best). These provide great resources for students who can't find a topic. There are even books out there that publish lists of ideas.

● Look at the list of the many different sciences on page 81, and pick one that interests you. Then try to narrow your science down to a topic. For example, say you find meteorology intriguing. Now, narrow your topic down by thinking about what elements of meteorology grab your attention: clouds, storms, weather patterns, and so on.

● Go to the library. Browse through the science section. Or check out the encyclopedias and magazines. Reference librarians are also great resources. You can ask them anything, and they'll help you find the answer.

● Read the newspaper. Current events can lead you to a great topic. Say you read an article about excessive flooding in your neighborhood, and one citizen blames the floods on the fact that all the trees around the neighborhood's river have been cleared. You could then devise a problem and an experiment that test the citizen's opinion.

● Ask any of your teachers (not just your science teacher) for advice and ideas. Science teachers aren't the only ones who wonder about the world.

Write down all of your possible ideas in your notebook. Narrow down possible topics until you have one that works for you.

An Eight-Week Schedule

Week #1
☐ Choose your topic.
☐ Organize your notebook.
☐ Ask questions.

Week #2
☐ Research your chosen topic.

Week #3
☐ Finish your research.
☐ Define your problem.
☐ Develop your hypothesis.
☐ Design your experiment.

Week #4
☐ Turn in an experiment summary to your teacher.
☐ Gather all needed materials for your experiment.
☐ Start your experiment.

Week #5
☐ Set up an outline for your project report.
☐ Continue your experiment.

☐ Begin collecting materials for your display.

Week #6
☐ Continue your experiment.
☐ Write the first draft of your project report.
☐ Sketch some designs for your display.

Week #7
☐ Finish your experiment.
☐ Revise list of materials needed for the experiment and the steps of the procedure, if necessary.
☐ Analyze your data, and draw your conclusions.
☐ Revise the project report.

Week #8
☐ Complete your display.
☐ Edit and type the final draft of the project report.
☐ Prepare for the fair.

5. Research Your Topic

After choosing a topic, you're ready to start your project research. You'll need to find as much information on your topic as you can so you'll not only understand your topic, but also so you can define your problem, develop a hypothesis, and design and conduct an experiment. Understanding your topic will make those steps a whole lot easier. Also, judges and teachers alike will be

impressed with your knowledge. You might even impress yourself. If, however, you're one of those people who would rather experience some crude form of medieval torture than do a little research, the fact that you've chosen a topic you care about increases the chances that you won't be comparing this research effort to having your fingernails pulled out. Just as you got the chance to choose your own topic, you also get to choose how you'll research your topic. Do libraries make you sleepy? Photocopy library materials and read them at home. Like computers? Use the Internet to find information. Enjoy talking to people? Contact scientists

and other professionals to help you with your research. No matter how organized you are, you'll run into blind alleys. Try not to get too frustrated. You won't find good information everywhere you look, but here are some suggestions to get you started:

● Write down in your notebook everything you already know about your topic. On a second page, write down all your questions about the topic and what you'd like to learn. These two lists will provide you with some focus as you start your research.

● With your lists in hand, do a topic search over the Internet. You may find people or associations dedicated to your topic, and many of them will have e-mail addresses. You may also find books you could buy (or find later at the library).

● Hit the library. Ask the reference librarian to get you started, or do your own topic research. Many libraries now have CD-roms that contain thousands of full-length articles you can search through. When looking through books that may or may not be helpful, check the table of contents and indexes to see if your topic is included. Also check out the library's encyclopedias, newspapers, and magazines.

● Seek out professionals, scientists, and others who may

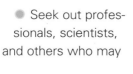

have information on your topic. You could write to them asking for information, e-mail them, or even call them to set up an interview. Most professionals love to help students, and the ones who don't will still probably help you once they hear how enthusiastic you are about the subject.

● Section off several pages of your notebook to organize all of the information you've accumulated. Write down names, sources, pages, titles, Web-site addresses, and a summary of each article or chapter used. Check with your teacher for advice on keeping a bibliography.

6. Fine-tune Your Topic

Once you've completed your research, it's time to use it. Your first step is to finalize your problem by turning it into a question that can be answered by conducting an experiment. Say, for example, you're interested in organic foods. That's a great topic, but it needs more focus; it's not a question or a problem yet. You could ask if there's a health benefit from eating organic vegetables instead of vegetables grown with chemical pesticides. However, after doing your research,

> **"R**esearch is the act of going up alleys to see if they are blind."
> –Plutarch, really old smart person

you realize that kind of experiment could take years to conduct, and you only have two months. You don't want to bite off more than you can chew. Also, remember that you don't want to choose a topic that will be too difficult to explore by yourself. Of course it's okay to ask for help when you're stuck, but you don't want to have to rely too heavily on other people. Anyway, what if you wanted to find out if organic vegetables *taste* better than conventionally grown vegetables? Now you're getting somewhere. Your question or problem could be "Do organic vegetables taste better than conventionally grown vegetables?" And that would be okay, but still not quite there, because your question or problem needs to be *open-ended*. That means your question should not be able to be answered simply by stating "yes" or "no." And this is THE KEY to the scientific method! Rewrite the question like this, "What effect do pesticides have on the taste of vegetables?" Or, "How do pesticides affect the taste of vegetables?" (See the box on the right for advice on using the words "affect" and "effect.") And then, you need to

ask yourself whether or not you could devise an experiment to answer the question. In this case, a blind taste test including several different tasters could give you the data you need to come up with a solution.

Finally, make sure you read all the science fair rules and guidelines before continuing with your project. Rules vary, but some common rules include:

● You can't use dangerous materials in your project, i.e., toxic, caustic, flammable, or explosive chemicals; harmful bacteria; ionizing radiation; high voltage/amperage electrical equipment; or

The Difference Between "Effect" and "Affect"

Nothing irks a teacher or judge more than a science fair participant who mixes up "effect" and "affect." Though both words can be either nouns or verbs, "effect" is usually used as a noun that means "consequence" or "result." "Affect" is usually used as a verb that means "to influence." If either of those words appears in your title, problem, or report, and you don't know which one to use, try putting the above definitions into the sentence. Only one should feel right. If you are still confused, have someone look over the sentence and help you.

improperly shielded electrical equipment.

● You can't do an experiment with animals that involves the animals' discomfort, pain, or death. Even if you want to do an experiment on an animal that won't hurt it, make sure to get permission from the science fair organizers before proceeding.

If you think you have a great topic but are not sure whether or not you're breaking any of the rules, ask the school's science fair coordinator or your science teacher.

IMPLEMENTING THE PLAN

If you've taken your time and planned well, then this is your payoff. These next steps will not be as scary and time consuming as you originally thought. Go ahead and pat yourself on the back. You deserve it. Now get back to work.

1. Develop Your Hypothesis

A hypothesis is your educated guess about the solution to your problem, based on previous knowledge (what you already know) and research. The experiment you design will either support your hypothesis or disprove it. Your hypothesis should be short and to the point, and it should clearly indicate what you plan to do or find out.

For example, you observed your mom's tomato plants in her garden last summer, and realized they weren't growing as quickly as your next-door neighbor's tomato plants. You asked your mom why she thinks this is the case, and she points out that she doesn't use any chemical fertilizers in her garden, though the next-door neighbor does. You decide to test this for

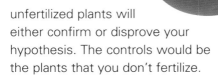

your science fair project. You narrow down your topic to "What is the effect of chemical fertilizers on the growth of tomato plants?" You research chemical fertilizers and are now ready to state your hypothesis. Since it's your hypothesis, use "I."

"I believe tomato plants will grow faster when chemically fertilized because..."

That's the first part of your hypothesis. The second part will relate facts from your personal observations and research that helped you decide on your hypothesis.

"...my neighbor's chemically fertilized tomato plants grew faster than my mother's unfertilized tomato plants. Also, research indicates that chemical fertilizers supply plants with essential nutrients that may be missing from the soil."

2. Design Your Experiment

Now it's time to develop an experiment that accurately tests your

---

Two atoms bump into each other while walking down the street. One says to the other,
"Are you all right?"
"No, I lost an electron!"
"Are you sure?"
"Yeah, I'm positive!"

---

hypothesis. Your experiment needs to be as simple as possible, because the more complicated the experiment, the more chance there is for error. The best way to see if an experiment will work is to define your *variables*. These include *anything* that can affect the outcome of the experiment (please notice the use of the word "affect"). The *independent variable* is the one thing that the experimenter purposely changes to see what happens. The *dependent variable* is what happens as a result of the change the experimenter makes. The variables that are not changed are the *controls*. Controls are needed to see what would happen under normal conditions—when you don't change anything at all. A little confused? Here's some help using the tomato experiment as an example:

You're ready to design your experiment, and you decide the best way to test your hypothesis is to grow some tomato plants in your living room and fertilize some of them and leave the rest of them alone. Then you'll compare the growth rates of the fertilized plants versus the unfertilized plants. For this experiment, the fertilizer is your independent variable. It's the change you're making to some of the tomato plants. The dependent variable is the measurement of the plants' heights. A difference in height between fertilized and unfertilized plants will either confirm or disprove your hypothesis. The controls would be the plants that you don't fertilize.

For a successful experiment, you must have only ONE independent variable. If you put your plants in different locations, water them at different times of the day and with different amounts of water, you won't be able to say that it was the fertilizer that caused a growth difference between the tomato plants. It could have been the location or the water. It's your primary responsibility to make sure you do everything in your power to control the environment so you can say that it was your independent variable that caused the difference.

As you develop your experiment, write out your steps, and check with your science teacher to make sure you only have one independent variable and that you have the proper controls for your experiment.

Here are the step-by-step instructions for the tomato experiment with the proper controls:

1. Purchase one packet of tomato seeds, 10 plant pots (same size), and one bag of potting soil. (To be even more careful, you could use seeds from one tomato.)

2. Label the pots 1 through 10.

3. Put the same amount of soil into each pot.

4. Place one seed exactly 1 inch (2.5 cm) into the soil of each pot.

5. Place the pots in the same sunny location.

6. Water the seeds with the same amount of water every other day for 10 days.

7. Add the same amount of fertilizer to pots 1 through 5.

8. Observe the plants for one month, and measure and record the growth of each plant.

9. Average the heights of the fertilized plants (pots 1 through 5) and then the heights of the unfertilized plants (pots 6 through 10).

10. Record any differences in the averages.

It's best to either repeat your experiment a number of times or to make sure you have more than one test subject in your experiment. An experiment comparing 1,000 tomato plants will be considered more convincing than an experiment comparing two tomato plants. This also minimizes human error. You won't be able to control every variable, so note any variables that you won't be able to control, but which may affect your outcome. If the tomato seeds you used for your experiment came from a

seed packet, there's no guarantee that these seeds came from the same tomato or even the same plant.

3. Conduct the Experiment

After you've written up your experiment's design, show it to your science teacher, because it will save

you a lot of time if you've made a mistake. Gather all of the materials needed for the experiment and follow your steps. As you conduct your experiment, record all your data in your notebook. Take detailed notes of your materials, measurements, observations, and thoughts. Every time you enter information in your journal, note the date, the time, and any other important information. Include as much information as possible. Take pictures or draw diagrams of your experiment. Also, remember that just because something happens once, that doesn't necessarily support or disprove your hypothesis.

Repeat your experiment. Then repeat it again.

4. Analyze Data and Draw Conclusions

After you've collected all your data and you feel confident you have enough, do any calculations that'll help you draw a conclusion. Make charts or graphs to help you. Then, the big question we've all been waiting for: do your results support or disprove your hypothesis? If your experiment doesn't support your hypothesis, don't get upset. It's actually pretty cool. In fact, sometimes it's even more interesting than if it did support it. Judges won't penalize you for disproving your own hypothesis, and they'll be quite impressed if you've thought of possibilities as to why your hypothesis wasn't supported by the experiment.

Your project conclusion is a short summary of your experiment's results and how they relate to your hypothesis. You can also add questions that came up as a result of your experiment. For example, you've completed your tomato plant experiment and calculated your results, and as expected, the tomato plants that were fertilized were bigger than the unfertilized plants. Your conclusion could be:

"As stated in my hypothesis, I believe that tomato plants grown with fertilizer will be bigger than tomato plants grown without fertilizer. My experiment supports my hypothesis. After 30 days of observations, the tomato plants grown with fertilizer averaged ½ inch (1.3 cm) taller than the plants grown without fertilizer. If I were to improve this experiment, I wouldn't use purchased potting soil for the experiment, since many potting soils already have added nutrients to help plants grow better. I believe I would have achieved more convincing results if I had used soil from my mother's garden."

5. Write the Project Report

The project report is the whole enchilada—your complete written record of your project neatly wrapped up. And, if you've followed this book's advice and kept detailed notes in your notebook every step of the way, your report will be a cinch because everything you need for the report will already be in the notebook.

In the report, you have to detail what you did, how you did it, why you did it, where you got your information from, and who helped out. Check with your science teacher for the order and content of the report.

Make sure it's typed, double-spaced, and bound (in a folder).

6. Showing Off

Ready to show off all of your hard work? Well, it's time to get ready for the actual science fair. At the science fair, you'll be given space on a table to display your experiment, and it's your job to tell the whole story of your project on that table in an interesting and eye-catching way. You want to show that you know what you're talking about and get the attention of judges with a display that is organized, neat, creative, and fun.

Your Checklist for Success #3:

Writing a Good Report

- [ ] I included a title page that lists the name of the project, my name, grade, and school.

- [ ] I devised a table of contents that lists what's in the report and what page everything's on.

- [ ] I included an abstract, which is a brief, one-page overview of the project. The abstract includes the title and a summary of the purpose, hypothesis, procedure, and results.

- [ ] My introduction states my purpose along with any information that led me to choose this topic.

- [ ] The list of materials and equipment needed for the experiment is included.

- [ ] The step-by-step description of my experiment's procedures, including all variables and how I measured and recorded what happened, is included.

- [ ] All of my data is included, along with all charts and graphs with short written summaries for each one.

- [ ] I have a conclusion that tells how I interpreted my results.

- [ ] My sources, including all written materials, as well as anyone I may have interviewed, are listed.

- [ ] I have an acknowledgments page, stating who helped me and how they helped.

The first thing you should do is choose a title for your project. Pick something short and to the point. If you can think of something witty, use it, but don't get hung up on it. For example, the tomato experiment could be called "The Tomato Race" or "An Unfair Advantage." All of your information will be displayed on a three-paneled display board. This is a large piece of cardboard (usually 48 x 36 inches [1.2 x .9 m] unfolded) that can stand by itself. You can usually find this cardboard in office supply stores. You can create your own, but make sure it's not bigger than what the science fair allows. On this board you will need to present the following:

- ▶ **Title**
- ▶ **Problem**
- ▶ **Hypothesis**
- ▶ **Abstract**
- ▶ **Experiment materials**
- ▶ **Experimental procedures**
- ▶ **Data**
- ▶ **Results**
- ▶ **Conclusion**

Each section should be computer generated, with the heading of each section big enough to see from a distance. The title should be bigger than the headings. Use stencils or a computer to create the title. Also display photographs of the procedure and results, and create attractive graphs and tables to show your data. For an added visual element to your display, you can cover your display with colored, self-adhesive shelf paper (the displays usually only come in black or white), and then you could place each of your sections on colored construction paper, leaving an attractive border around the edges. You could also use light colored paper to type your sections on. When you're ready, first lay the board on the floor and arrange the information so that it looks good. Get family members or friends to look at it and give advice. Make sure your display doesn't look too crowded and that there are no wide-open spaces—everything should be placed evenly on the board. Use rubber cement to paste your information to the board.

You'll have some space on the table in front of the display for your written report, notebook, any models made for the experiment, and anything else you can include that represents your experiment, such as a couple of the tomato plants. Make sure to check the science fair rules concerning items you're not allowed to bring. Such lists usually include animals, fungi, liquids, chemicals, or anything that could possibly hurt someone.

7. Here Comes the Judge

If you're part of a judged science fair, the judges may look at all the projects while you're not in the room, and then, later, interview you in front of your project. Most science fair judges use a point system to judge projects, and science fair judging varies from competition to competition. If you've followed all the steps in the last couple of chapters, you're probably quite knowledgeable about your topic and experiment. In fact, you may even know more about your topic than the judges. So, relax. The night before the science fair, you can ask your parents to pretend they're judges. Have them ask you questions, and practice your responses. But don't feel like you have to memorize your project. Have confidence in your work and in yourself. Answer questions thoroughly, and don't be afraid to say you don't know an answer to a question. Judges respect that. They may ask how you'll continue your project. Mention interesting questions that came up as you worked on the project. Remember, the judges are not there to "get" you. They simply want to reward students who have worked hard, learned a lot, and done a great job.

And that's it! You're done. Feels good, doesn't it!?

Good luck with your project, and remember, being a winner isn't simply about getting a ribbon at the end of the science fair. It's about being proud, really proud, of the time and work and sweat you put into your project. You're also a winner not only because you came out of the whole experience still alive and breathing, but because you're a little bit smarter, perhaps a bit more curious, and you're that much closer to being a true explorer of the world around you...a scientist.

> "Reserve your right to think, for even to think wrongly is better than not to think at all." –Hypathia, mathematician and natural philosopher (see page 105)

Your Checklist for Success #4:
What the Judges Look For

- [ ] My project shows original thinking and investigation of an original idea. (You won't get a lot of points for a project that has been done every year for the last 30 years.)

- [ ] My project is well organized.

- [ ] I show that I've used the scientific method and have defined my variables and controls.

- [ ] I did my research and documented it.

- [ ] I used a notebook to collect data and research.

- [ ] I worked carefully on the experiment.

- [ ] I presented my materials to the judges in an organized and knowledgeable way and answered questions accurately.

- [ ] I used tables, graphs, and illustrations in interpreting data.

- [ ] I know what I'm talking about, and I understand the science involved in my experiment.

- [ ] I have a display that's attractive, well labeled, and easily understood.

- [ ] I have a complete and comprehensive report.

The Projects!

The projects in the next three chapters explore three major branches of science: biology, physical science, and chemistry. In each chapter you'll find projects with varying degrees of difficulty; the easier projects come first, and they get more challenging as each chapter continues. If the project requires adult supervision or assistance, there will be an **ADULT SUPERVISION REQUIRED** bullet in the upper right-hand corner of the project page. Take this seriously. Some experiments require the use of stoves, drills, acids, and chemicals, and even though science is fun, it also pays to be cautious.

Each project is broken down into different sections, which are explained below.

● The **PROBLEM/PURPOSE** asks the question that the experiment seeks to answer. Please note that there is no section for hypothesis. It's your job to do the research and come up with your own hypothesis.

● The **EXPERIMENT SUMMARY** gives you a basic idea of how you'll conduct the experiment.

● **WHAT YOU NEED** is your supply list of everything you'll need to do the experiment. Please note that each list tells you how many volunteers or plant seeds, etc., you'll need for a valid experiment. Remember, however, that the more trials you perform, the more valid your results will be. So, find more volunteers or use more plants whenever possible.

● The **EXPERIMENTAL PROCEDURE** provides step-by-step instructions for doing the experiment.

● The **CONCLUSION** gives you questions, advice, and general assistance to help you find your conclusion.

● For many of the projects you can **TAKE A CLOSER LOOK** and delve deeper into the topic. Sometimes this section provides more information about the conclusion, and other times it includes facts, tidbits, and other information that can help you with your research.

● **WHAT ELSE YOU CAN DO** shows related ideas and other experiments to try for many of the experiments.

● When there's a cool idea for your display, it's included in **DISPLAY TIPS**.

Read the whole project before deciding it's the project for you. Use the Take a Closer Look section (if available) to help you start your research. Also, make sure you can get all the materials you need. If the What You Need section mentions that you need a swimming pool, make sure you can find one you can use before continuing with the project.

What are you waiting for? Turn the page already!

Simply Alarming!

Say for some strange, awful reason, you have to wake up tomorrow at 5:00 a.m. How will you do it? Most likely you'll set your alarm clock. But what if you simply set your internal alarm clock? Yes, scientists believe that we have internal alarm clocks that can help us wake up. Here's an experiment that tests whether or not simply telling yourself to wake up at a certain hour actually works.

PROBLEM/PURPOSE

What is the effect of our internal clocks on awakening at an unusual hour?

EXPERIMENT
SUMMARY

Using 12 volunteers, six with alarm clocks and six without, you'll test their abilities to wake up at an unusually early time.

WHAT YOU
NEED

▶ **12 really willing volunteers who don't normally wake up at 5:00 a.m.***

▶ **12 notebooks**

▶ **6 alarm clocks**

Set up the experiment for a week when you're off from school. You don't want your volunteers falling asleep in class!

EXPERIMENTAL PROCEDURE

1. Instruct six volunteers to set their alarm clocks for 5:00 a.m. for one week.

2. Instruct the rest of the volunteers to wake up at 5:00 a.m. without the aid of an alarm clock. They must be awake long enough to write down in their notebook the exact time they woke up.

3. Have each volunteer record the time they woke up each day of the week.

4. Compare the success/failure rate of the alarm clock (control) group to the group who had no alarm clocks.

CONCLUSION

What strategies did the experimental group come up with for waking up without an alarm clock? Did anyone picture an actual clock in their head, or did they simply tell themselves to wake up? Were their attempts successful? Did the volunteers without the alarm clocks improve throughout the week? Did they find themselves waking up earlier than asked to? How did their attempts compare to the control group as the week progressed? Show bar graphs that compare the success rate of the volunteers. Make sure to point out any variations as the week progressed. In other words, don't be satisfied by simply stating that the experimental group did better or worse than the control group. Check your data for any signs that the experimental group got better at waking up at 5 a.m. each day of the experiment.

TAKE A CLOSER LOOK

● Hormones, the chemicals that transfer information and instructions between cells, may help some people wake up when they need to without an alarm clock. There are special hormones that help a body prepare for stressful events, which include waking up. During sleep, the amounts of these hormones gradually increase and then begin really increasing about one hour before waking up. So scientists conclude that simply expecting to wake up at a certain time sets an internal alarm clock that continues ticking when you're asleep, and the hormone surge is the alarm that wakes you up.

WHAT ELSE YOU CAN DO

● Biological clocks are internal systems that help humans and all living things live in harmony with life's rhythms, such as the seasons. Circadian rhythms are daily rhythms, or what you do each and every day. What do you think would happen to your daily rhythm if there was no sunrise? Study an insect's normal behavior during a one-week period, and then compare it to the insect's behavior when deprived of sunlight for one week. How does the insect's circadian rhythm change?

The Video Game Advantage

There are some who say that kids who play video games develop great reaction time, to the point where those who play A LOT of video games may be well suited for careers as military aviators. Just how much video game playing does it take to develop a quicker reaction time?

PROBLEM/PURPOSE

What effect does playing video games have on reaction time?

EXPERIMENT SUMMARY

You'll perform a simple test using only a ruler to see if students who play a lot of video games have a reaction time advantage over students who don't play video games.

WHAT YOU NEED

- ▶ Copies of a video game survey (see survey on right)
- ▶ 30 volunteers (or as many students as you can get)
- ▶ Ruler

EXPERIMENTAL PROCEDURE

1. Your best bet for finding volunteers for this project is to survey your class. See the sample survey on the right. Ask your teacher to photocopy the survey for you, and then hand it out to your classmates to fill out. Make sure they put their names on the sheets.

2. Once you've received the surveys back, organize them according to their responses so you have four groups with the same number of participants.

3. Have your first volunteer stand up. Hold the ruler near the end by the highest number, and let it hang down. Ask the volunteer to place his hand directly below the ruler as if he was going to grab it. Make sure he's not touching the ruler.

4. Tell the volunteer you're going to drop the ruler at some point within the next 10 seconds, and that he should catch the ruler between his thumb and finger as fast as he can.

5. Drop the ruler, and record where he caught it (you can use inches or centimeters). Measure at the top of the hand.

6. Repeat the test five times, and record the average. Make sure that each time you drop the ruler you vary the time in which you let it go. If you let it go after 5 seconds each time, your volunteer will anticipate the drop.

7. Repeat steps 3 through 6 for each of the volunteers.

CONCLUSION

Once you've completed the experiment, take the averages of each of the four groups of volunteers, and calculate the average length each of the four groups caught the ruler. The higher the number, the longer it took for them to catch the ruler.

Video Game Survey

Name: _____

Please circle one answer for each of the two questions.

1. How many hours a week do you spend playing video games?
   1) 0 hours
   2) 1 to 5 hours
   3) 6 to 15 hours
   4) 16 to 25 hours or more

2. Would you be willing to participate in a fun science experiment?
   1) Yes
   2) No

Which of the four groups showed an advantage? Did extensive video game playing affect the outcome?

TAKE A CLOSER LOOK

● When your eyes see the ruler move, that information has to travel to your brain, which then sends a signal to your hand to grab it. And talk about fast service! If a volunteer caught the ruler at a length of 2 inches (5.1 cm), their reaction time was one-tenth of a second. If, on the other hand, they caught the ruler at 12 inches (30.5 cm), then their reaction time was still only one-quarter of a second!

WHAT ELSE YOU CAN DO

● Do the same experiment comparing athletes and nonathletes, or boys and girls, etc.

● Scientists state that reaction time is greatly increased after a night of very little to no sleep. On a nonschool night, invite some friends over and do the ruler experiment when they arrive. Stay up really late, and then get up early the next morning (make sure you have your parents' permission to do this!), and redo the experiment again. Compare the results.

Food for the Beans

Plants dig water. Without it, they die. But what would happen if you decided to water your plants with cola or orange juice? They contain water, right? Let's check it out....

PROBLEM/PURPOSE

How will different liquids affect the growth rates of bean seeds?

EXPERIMENT SUMMARY

Six bean seeds will be planted in the same-sized pots and then watered with different substances. Over a two-month period, you'll record the growth of each of the plants and compare them with the plant receiving plain water.

WHAT YOU NEED

▶ **Potting soil**
▶ **12 planters**
▶ **12 small lima bean seeds**
▶ **Water**
▶ **Vinegar and water solution (25 percent vinegar)**
▶ **Baking soda and water solution (25 percent baking soda)**
▶ **Orange juice**
▶ **Milk**
▶ **Cola**
▶ **Ruler**

EXPERIMENTAL PROCEDURE

1. Plant your seeds in the pots. Make sure you put them all in the dirt at the same depth (1 inch [2.5 cm] preferred).

2. Label each pot with what you're going to water each seed with. You'll water two plants with each substance, so label the first two plants "water," the next two plants "vinegar and water solution," and so on.

3. Place each pot in the same sunny location.

4. Water the seeds every other day with the same amount of liquid (this is important). Record when the seeds have sprouted, and then begin measuring height and observing the general health of each of the growing plants. General health could include whether or not any plants are dying or if leaves are turning yellow or falling off.

5. Observe the plant growth for at least two months (or as long as you can).

CONCLUSION

Did any of the substances produce taller and healthier plants than the water? Did any plants start off strongly and then begin to wither or die? Did any seeds fail to germinate? What do you think happened to those plants? Did the acidic or alkaline substances perform well or poorly?

TAKE A CLOSER LOOK

● Plants don't need much from us to thrive. Some water and some sunlight and they're usually set, so introducing too much of any other substance (especially one that is very alkaline or acidic) will alter the way plants take up the minerals they need to survive. Also, plants usually thrive in a soil that's fairly neutral, and adding substances they don't need could eventually ruin the soil in the pot.

Take a Closer Look:
What's REALLY in the Food You Eat

Your stomach starts rumbling, so you head to the kitchen for something to eat. Do you ever wonder what's really in that snack? What exactly do the gibberish-sounding words on food labels mean? Take a closer look.

Some people may prefer chocolate or vanilla ice cream, but have you ever heard of anyone who liked seaweed ice cream? *Carrageenan*, extracted from seaweed, is found in many ice creams. It's used to prevent those pesky ice crystals from growing too large. In chocolate milk, carrageenan stops the cocoa from settling on the bottom. *Alginates*, also extracted from seaweed, are used to thicken salad dressings.

If you think seaweed and ice cream are a strange combination, try hair and bread. Derived from human hair, the ingredient *cysteine* (or *cystine*) is found in about 5 percent of breads. Cheese also contains ingredients from unlikely body parts. In order for the dairy product to coagulate, cheese is sometimes made with the enzyme *rennet*, which is obtained from cows' stomachs.

Does your dessert or fat-free yogurt jiggle? Chances are it contains *gelatin*. Gelatin is made from the bones, skins, hooves, and tendons of cows and other animals. Yummy!

Got *carmine*? That's a food coloring made from beetles.

Sometimes, foods even share ingredients with non-food products. Some chewing gums contain *dercolytes*—the same adhesive used in tapes and labels. The next time you're out of gum, you can just reach for the nearest tape dispenser (ha, ha...please don't)!

If you're a little grossed out by the strange ingredients you didn't even know you were eating, just be thankful you're not the family pet. Pet food is processed from the leftover animal parts not fit for human consumption. These include bones, blood, intestines, lungs, and ligaments.

Bon appétit!

"You!"

"What's for lunch?"

What's That Smell? Oh, It's Me!

Even though we humans don't rely on our sense of smell as much as say, dogs or mice, scientists have long known that odors and subliminal scents—also known as *pheromones*—may influence how we develop, learn, and bond with our parents. They may even help us decide who we fall in love with! Here's an experiment that will help you figure out whether or not we have individual scents.

How accurately can moms identify their children's clothing using only the sense of smell?

EXPERIMENT SUMMARY

You and five friends of the same gender will wear identical T-shirts to bed for five nights. Then you'll collect the shirts, label them, and test if the moms can accurately identify their child's shirt using their sense of smell.

WHAT YOU NEED

▸ 6 test subjects (you and 5 friends of the same gender)

▸ 6 brand-new T-shirts (make sure they're all the same color and size)

▸ 6 plastic bags that "lock"

▸ 6 markers, different colors

EXPERIMENTAL PROCEDURE

1. Choose your test group.

2. Take each shirt out of its wrapping, and use the markers to place a different colored mark on the tag of each one. This will help you remember whose shirt is whose.

3. Place each T-shirt in a bag labeled with the subject's name. Create a list of the volunteers' names along with the colors of their tags.

4. Ask each subject to sleep in the T-shirt for five nights. Make sure

they don't use any type of scented lotion, perfume, etc. Also make sure the moms don't see the color-code on the tag of the shirts.

5. After the five-day period, travel to each of the test subjects' homes and place the shirts on a table. Ask the subject's mom to smell each shirt and indicate which one she believes is her child's. Record the results.

CONCLUSION

If your data is inconclusive (if some moms could but others couldn't indicate their child's shirt), try redoing the experiment with more test subjects. The more subjects you include, the more data you'll accumulate, and the better chance you'll have of coming up with a result.

TAKE A CLOSER LOOK

● The chemical *pheromone*, which gives each person their unique body smell, is not as powerful as the smell of your mom's meatloaf, but don't automatically assume pheromones don't pack a punch. Pheromones are produced by animals in order to affect how other animals behave, and may be the most ancient form of animal communication. For example, the next time you see two dogs meeting for the first time, watch what they do: they smell each other. Even ants use pheromones to keep track of food, to warn of nearby enemies, and to tell others to run away. Finally, humans also use pheromones. Within several days after birth, infants who breastfeed can tell their own mother from another person simply through smell. And even though we all have distinct smells, odors of family members will be similar, while identical twins will have identical odors!

WHAT ELSE YOU CAN DO

● Compare moms' success rates against dads' success rates.

● Test whether or not parents can tell the difference between the smells of all their kids.

● Can you pick out your own smell?

Time for Your Veggies

There's a lot of controversy surrounding the use of organic foods versus foods grown with the use of chemical pesticides. Are organic foods better for us? What effect do pesticides have on us? In this experiment you'll address a simpler question: which taste better?

PROBLEM/PURPOSE

How does the taste of organic vegetables compare to the taste of conventionally grown vegetables?

EXPERIMENT SUMMARY

You'll conduct various taste tests involving raw, cooked, and canned vegetables that were grown both organically and conventionally.

WHAT YOU NEED

- **25 volunteers**
- **25 cups of water**
- **Raw organic cherry tomatoes**
- **Raw conventionally grown cherry tomatoes**
- **Organic carrots, sliced and steamed**
- **Regular carrots, sliced and steamed**
- **Canned organic corn, cooked**
- **Canned conventional corn, cooked**
- **75 photocopied questionnaires**
- **3 pens**

EXPERIMENTAL PROCEDURE

1. Set up taste-test stations so the volunteers can taste each vegetable. Place 25 copies of the questionnaire (see sample on the following page) at the station. Label the vegetables in each station "Vegetable A" and "Vegetable B." Make sure you don't tell the volunteers what your experiment is on. Also, if you notice a remarkable difference in the look of the vegetables, consider blindfolding your volunteers.

2. Have each volunteer visit the stations and taste the vegetables, sipping the water between each tasting.

3. After visiting a station, have the volunteer choose one of the responses on the questionnaire.

4. Once the experiment is done, tabulate the results and chart the responses.

CONCLUSION

After collecting the questionnaires, figure out how many volunteers preferred the organic or conventional vegetables for each station. Create a pie chart showing what percentages preferred the organic

vegetable, the conventionally grown vegetable, or showed no preference. Then combine your percentages for all three stations and create another pie chart. Did the percentages point to a clear favorite? Did different stations produce different preferences?

TAKE A CLOSER LOOK

● Organic meat and dairy farming is the raising of animals whose feed and care don't include hormones, antibiotics, or other artificial chemicals; it also includes allowing animals sufficient range of movement and sunlight.

● More than 18 million acres are now devoted to certified organic agriculture in 130 nations, yet that means that only 4 percent of farmers are growing organic foods.

● In order to be considered organic, farmers must grow produce for

An airplane spraying pesticides on crops

three years without using synthetic pesticides or chemicals.

WHAT ELSE YOU CAN DO

● Taste tests are fun experiments to conduct and they usually don't take too long. You can compare different brands of the same foods or compare generic brands versus name brands of the same foods.

● Many food items now boast less salt, sugar, and fat. How is taste affected when ingredients that are usually associated with good-tasting products are removed?

● Try conducting a taste test comparing many food

items, such as cookies, ice cream, sodas, etc., with their reduced-fat counterparts.

● Genetically engineered food may be the wave of the future in many parts of the world. Research what companies are doing to grow vegetables that have pesticides already in them.

DISPLAY TIPS

● Have a sample of some of the vegetables you tested for the judges. Don't forget the napkins.

The Questionnaire

Name: _____

Station #: _____

Circle one of the following:

A) I preferred Vegetable A.

B) I preferred Vegetable B.

C) I found no difference between A or B.

Ah...Refreshing!

It seems that chewing-gum commercials almost always claim that their gum is "cool and refreshing," but is your mouth really cooling off with all that chewing? Here's a fun experiment for which you'll easily find volunteers.

PROBLEM/PURPOSE

What effect does chewing mint-flavored gum have on the temperature of a person's mouth?

EXPERIMENT SUMMARY

You'll record the mouth temperatures of 15 volunteers, and then break them up into three groups who'll be chewing either mint-flavored gum, nonmint-flavored gum, or nothing. After chewing, temperatures will be taken again and compared to pre-chewing temperatures.

WHAT YOU NEED

▶ **15 volunteers**
▶ **15 oral thermometers (have each of your volunteers bring one)**
▶ **5 pieces of mint-flavored chewing gum**
▶ **5 pieces of cinnamon-flavored chewing gum**

EXPERIMENTAL PROCEDURE

1. Take the temperature of each participant before chewing. Record your data. You should ask your volunteers to keep their mouths still (in other words: no talking) for five minutes before the experiment. Also, in order to accurately record all temperatures, you should be the person who reads the thermometer and makes sure it's being used correctly. Ask a parent to help if you don't know how to use one of the thermometers (some of them are tricky).

2. Split the volunteers into three groups of five people each. Give each member in group 1 one piece of mint-flavored gum. Give each member in group number 2 one piece of cinnamon-flavored gum (make sure it's the same size as the mint-flavored gum—a much larger or smaller piece of gum may vary the results). Don't give the third group any gum at all.

3. Tell all three groups to start chewing (even the group with no gum!).

4. After two minutes, take each person's temperature and record it. Have them resume chewing.

5. When another two minutes have passed, have each person throw out their gum. Immediately take their temperatures and record them.

6. Wait five minutes (ask your participants to keep their mouths still) and record each person's temperature again.

7. Compare the temperatures from each recording.

8. Ask each volunteer to describe how their mouths felt while chewing. Compare their answers to the data.

9. You may want to do this experiment one group at a time, in order to give you enough time to read the temperatures without letting a lot of time pass between data recordings. Or, you can stagger the starting times of the chewing in order to get all your data quickly without having mouth temperature change dramatically while you're trying to record the data.

CONCLUSION

Did the volunteers feel like their mouths were getting hotter or cooler while chewing the gum? How did this compare with the actual temperatures you measured? Was there a difference in the way people chewed the gum, and how did it seem to compare to the degree that their mouths changed temperature? What was the average change in temperature? Graph the changes in temperature for each participant. You can chart the before and after temperatures in a bar graph, or plot each of the three temperatures you measured per person onto graph paper.

TAKE A CLOSER LOOK

● Chewing involves the tongue, jaw, and cheek muscles, and it draws blood to those areas. Increased blood flow and muscular activity naturally produce heat in the part of the body that's involved.

● A calorie is the unit of measurement for heat, and some foods require more energy to chew them than calories they contain. For example, a stalk of celery contains approximately five calories but the average person burns up to 95 calories just from chewing and digesting it!

WHAT ELSE YOU CAN DO

● Try this experiment with different flavors of gum and compare the temperature changes. Or try it with different shapes of gum. Will a big wad of gum provide different results when compared to a thin stick? What about chewing gum versus bubble gum?

● Compare the temperature of a person's mouth after chewing a hot pepper and then after chewing a stick of mint gum.

● Watch a lot of television and pay particular attention to the advertisements. What are these commercials claiming? Is that product really the best, most awesome, hottest, coolest, fastest, easiest...? It's up to you to set the record straight.

"My advice for any student embarking on a science fair project is: don't procrastinate. It slows you down in the long run and agitates you a whole lot. Also, take the time for accurate and adequate notes. And, be patient when doing an experiment. You can't just expect everything to work perfectly on the first try. It's worth every minute you put into your project when you reach the end."
–Mattie Horine, 7th grader

The Nose Knows

You're sick, and you know that spoonful of medicine is going to taste awful. You cringe, but it's of no use. As a last-ditch effort you hold your nose. But, will it help?

PROBLEM/PURPOSE

How does smell affect taste?

EXPERIMENT SUMMARY

You'll select several foods and perform a blind taste test with a twist: you'll use a blindfold and nose clips so participants won't be able to see or smell what they're eating.

WHAT YOU NEED

- ▶ 15 volunteers (make sure they don't have colds or allergies to foods)
- ▶ Blindfold
- ▶ Nose clip (the kind people use for swimming)
- ▶ Equal-sized bits of: apples, onions, chocolate, cheese, and strawberries
- ▶ Toothpicks

EXPERIMENTAL PROCEDURE

1. Decide where you'll hide your taste-test items prior to the arrival of your volunteers.

2. Test your volunteers one at a time. The more volunteers you find, the more valid your results.

3. Blindfold your volunteer and ask him or her to put on the nose clip. Feed the apple bits to the volunteer. Ask if he or she can identify the food. Record the response. Repeat with the rest of the food items.

4. Remove the nose plug and feed the apple bits to the volunteer. Ask if he or she can identify the food. Record the response. Repeat with the rest of the food items.

5. Follow the same procedure with each of the volunteers.

Note: If you believe the texture of the different food items is affecting your volunteers' responses, get a parent's help and puree the food in a food processor.

CONCLUSION

What were your volunteers' success rates in identifying the foods with the nose clips on? How did their success rates compare to their success after the nose clips were removed? Was there a particular food that most volunteers guessed correctly? What could be a possible cause?

TAKE A CLOSER LOOK

● Most people with a cold complain they can't taste food; they're wrong. The sense of taste is working normally; it's the sense of smell that's not working correctly. The *olfactory* system, the system that enables us to smell, works alongside your taste buds.

Time to Take Your Temperature

Your internal body temperature is normally about 98.6°F (37°C), but does your temperature change at all during the day?

PROBLEM/PURPOSE

How does a person's body temperature vary during the day?

EXPERIMENT SUMMARY

You'll take your temperature every hour from the time you wake up to when you're about to go to sleep. You'll do this for three days, and plot the temperatures on graph paper. After three days you'll compare the temperatures to see if there are any patterns.

WHAT YOU NEED

▶ **Oral digital thermometer (make sure you know how to use it)**

▶ **Wristwatch**

▶ **Graph paper**

▶ **Pencil**

EXPERIMENTAL PROCEDURE

1. On the first day of the experiment, take your temperature as soon as you wake up. Measure the temperature to the nearest tenth of a degree. Record the time and temperature in your notebook.

2. Repeat this every hour until you go to bed. You might want to find a watch with an alarm you can set every hour so you don't forget. Don't eat or drink anything right before you take your temperature, and make sure you take your temperature the same way every time to avoid mistakes.

3. Each time you record your temperature, also write down your activities during the previous hour.

4. Chart your body temperature and the time on the graph paper for each day of the experiment. Use the x-axis for "Time of Day" and y-axis for "Body Temperature."

CONCLUSION

Once you've graphed your results, record the high and low temperatures for each day and write down the difference between the two. How much of a difference is there between the high and low temperatures? What patterns emerged after three days of testing? Was there a temperature change after certain events, such as a shower, a sporting event, a difficult

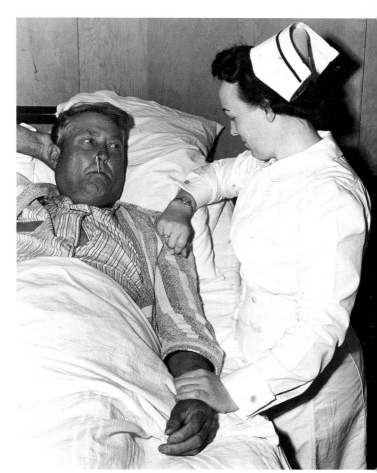

test? Does your temperature change as you get ready for bed? What conclusions can you draw about how temperature changes in the course of a day?

TAKE A CLOSER LOOK

● When we eat, the food is converted into protein, carbohydrates, and fat, and energy is released in the form of heat (this is the process of *metabolism*). This is how we maintain our body temperature. Strenuous exercise keeps the muscles moving, and active muscles convert food faster, so more heat is given off, which increases body temperature.

● One way to keep muscles active is to shiver. Shivering increases the metabolism and helps warm the body. Plus, goose bumps decrease the amount of surface (skin) that could lose heat.

● And what happens when we get too hot? We sweat and perhaps even pant. Both of these help regulate temperature when things get a little too hot.

● Your actual temperature will likely vary depending on the time of day, the level of activity, and your health. In fact, normal body temperature can vary up to 2° in a day.

● The highest human temperature recorded was 115°F (46°C). The lowest was 57°F (14°C).

● Here are the average body temperatures of some animals:
▶Sparrow: 105.8°F (41°C)
▶Rabbit: 101.3°F (38.5°C)
▶Owl: 104.4°F (40.2°C)
▶Ostrich: 102.6°F (39.2°C)

● Animals that hibernate conserve energy by lowering their body temperature. For example, the temperature of an opossum falls from 95°F (35°C) to 51°F (10.6°C) when hibernating.

● Cold-blooded animals, such as reptiles and amphibians, can't generate much of their own heat, but must obtain it from their environment.

WHAT ELSE YOU CAN DO

● If you happen to get sick, you can test your temperature change throughout the sickness. (Hey, you probably have nothing better to do!) Record the times you take medication, and chart how medication changes temperature as well.

● Ask your school nurse to check your blood pressure throughout one day, and record any changes.

● Compare daily temperature changes in boys and girls.

DISPLAY TIPS

● Create a large graph to show your daily temperature fluctuations.

Take a Closer Look:
Science Math

To find a percentage, simply divide the number by the number of trials then multiply by 100. For example, say you want to know the percentage of students who scored 80 or above on a science test. Add up the number of students who scored 80 or above (let's say 13) and suppose there are 28 students in the class. 13 ÷ 28 x 100 = 46.4 percent. So roughly 46 percent of all students in the class scored 80 or above.

Get a Grip

Believe it or not, magnets may have energizing and restorative effects on the human body. In fact, astronauts rely on magnets sewn into their suits to help keep them healthy when they venture into space away from the earth's natural magnetic field. Try this experiment to see what effect magnets have on you.

A dynamometer

PROBLEM/PURPOSE

What effect will magnets have on grip strength?

EXPERIMENT SUMMARY

With 20 volunteers you will compare the effect magnets have on grip strength for each individual.

WHAT YOU NEED

▶ **20 volunteers**
▶ **Elbow brace**
▶ **Health magnet in elbow brace**
▶ **Refrigerator magnet**
▶ **Dynamometer***

* This is a hand-held strength gauge that can be found at medical supply stores or over the Internet. You might also be able to borrow one from a physical therapist or chiropractor.

EXPERIMENTAL PROCEDURE

1. Before beginning your experiment, have each of your test subjects practice squeezing the dynamometer so that you and they become familiar with how it works.

2. Strap the plain (without magnet) elbow brace on the dominant arm of the first subject.

3. Ask the subject to squeeze the dynamometer with their dominant hand for a count of three.

4. Record the dynamometer measurement.

5. Repeat steps 2 through 4 two more times.

6. Wrap the health magnet brace around the elbow of the subject's arm you just tested.

7. Wait five minutes.

8. With the health magnet strapped around the subject's elbow, repeat steps 2 through 4 three times.

Feeling good...with magnets!

9. Repeat the test with a refrigerator magnet fastened to the plain elbow brace.

CONCLUSION

Examine the readings you recorded from the dynamo-meter for each person. Take an average of the three readings without magnets and compare this to the average of the three readings with the health magnet and with the refrigerator magnet. Did the average grip strength go up, down, or stay the same when the magnets were introduced? What is the greatest amount of change you noticed among the individual results? How did the health magnet compare to the refrigerator magnet?

TAKE A CLOSER LOOK

● The subject of magnets as a tool for health and physical recovery is controversial, partially because many of the success stories are based on personal experiences and there have been few scientific trials.

But NASA seems to believe in the theory that humans need a steady dose of magnetic energy for health. Astronauts used to feel really sick after returning from their journeys into space where the earth's magnetic force was diminished. Magnets have been installed in space suits to maintain a healthy level of magnetic influence on astronauts as they drift out of Earth's natural magnetic grasp.

● Here on Earth, proponents of magnets suggest that concrete, steel, and the various forms of radiation and electrical currents that surround us can interfere with Earth's natural magnetic field. Specially designed health magnets are recommended to restore a natural magnetic influence on the human body. Furthermore, those who are trained in the use of magnets for health believe that magnets can speed healing and affect the body by increasing circulation and essentially drawing more nutrients to the tissues near the mag-

net sites. The more blood that's brought to an injured area, the faster the involved cells will be replenished and the tissues will heal.

● Magnetars are neutron stars with unusually solid crusts. They produce the most powerful magnetic forces in the universe. Here is a quick comparison of sources of magnetic fields:

▶ Earth (strong enough to deflect a compass) = .6 Gauss

▶ A common refrigerator magnet = 100 Gauss (see what happens when you put one near your compass)

▶ Sunspots = 1000 Gauss

▶ Magnetar = 1,000,000,000,000,000 Gauss

● A "Gauss" is the unit of measurement for magnetism. According to scientists, anything over 1 billion Gauss of magnetic strength would rearrange the atoms and molecules in your body and result in instant death! The strongest magnetic field created in a laboratory was a mere 400,000 Gauss. A lot of zippers were probably missing after that experiment!

DISPLAY TIPS

● The results of this experiment are perfect for graphing. Try plugging your numbers into a computer program to make a bar graph to compare the averages for each individual. Provide samples of the sorts of magnetic devices that are available as health and healing products.

Are You Left Out or Right On?

Most likely, nearly all of your friends are right-handed, meaning they write, eat, and throw with their right hand. In fact, only about 13 percent of the world's population is left-handed. This relative lack of lefties has left scientists pondering what causes someone to be left-handed when much of the world is right-handed; however, in this experiment, you'll test whether the hand you use most often also determines which foot, eye, and ear is preferred.

PROBLEM/PURPOSE

How does one's handedness affect foot, eye, and ear preference?

EXPERIMENT SUMMARY

You'll test decidedly right-handed and left-handed students in a number of quick experiments to determine if they also have a dominant foot, eye, and ear.

WHAT YOU NEED

- ▶ **15 right-handed volunteers**
- ▶ **15 left-handed volunteers (you may have to search your whole school to find enough)**
- ▶ **Soccer ball**
- ▶ **Cardboard tube**
- ▶ **Toy bow and arrow set**
- ▶ **Small cardboard box**
- ▶ **Packing peanuts**
- ▶ **Tape**

EXPERIMENTAL PROCEDURE

Finding out who's right-handed is easier than finding out who's left-handed. The best way to determine handedness before the experiment is to ask each potential volunteer which hand they use to write, cut, throw, and eat with. Right-handed people will probably answer that they use their right hand for all of those activities, whereas left-handed people may only do some of them with their left hand. If they do three out of four with their left hand, consider them left-handed (many left-handed people are instructed to write with their right hand by parents and teachers).

TESTING FOOT PREFERENCE

1. Have each volunteer stand in front of a soccer ball. Ask them to kick it. Record which foot each of your volunteers used to kick the ball.

2. Have each volunteer stand at the bottom of the stairs. Ask them to climb the stairs, and note which foot they used to begin their climb.

3. Record which foot each volunteer used for both activities. If a volunteer used the same foot for both, then consider that a preference. If a volunteer used different feet for the two activities, consider that no preference.

TESTING EYE PREFERENCE

1. Ask each volunteer to look through the cardboard tube. Record which eye they used. If you have access to a telescope, use that instead.

2. Ask each volunteer to pick up the bow and arrow and aim it at an object across the room. Record which eye remains open.

3. Record which eye each volunteer used for both activities. If a volunteer used the same eye for both, then consider that a preference. If a volunteer used different eyes for the two activities, consider that no preference.

TESTING EAR PREFERENCE

1. Ask each volunteer to put their ear up to a wall to see if they can hear what's going on in the next room. Record which ear they put up to the wall.

2. Place several packing peanuts in a cardboard box and tape the box shut.

3. Ask each volunteer to shake the box to identify what's inside the box. Record which ear they bring the box up to. If they don't bring it up to an ear, suggest that they do so.

4. Record which ear each volunteer used for both activities. If a volunteer used the same ear for both, then consider that a preference. If a volunteer used different

ears for the two activities, consider that no preference.

CONCLUSION

Chart your results. Use the chart on the following page, or devise your own.

According to your results, did a higher percentage of one handedness also show signs of dominance in the three tested areas than the other handedness? Which handedness had more volunteers show no preference in one or more test

area? Did either handedness show a preference for the other side? Did any of the experiments point to a body part showing no preference at all (under 50 percent)?

TAKE A CLOSER LOOK

● The reasons why we prefer to use a certain hand (as well as eye, ear, or foot) are not completely understood. In fact, scientists aren't even sure why the majority of the world's population is right-handed, though many agree that it's a combination of heredity (your genes) and environment (circumstances in your life). Scientists are also confused as to why right-handed

Body Part	% of right-handed volunteers who preferred their right...	% of right-handed volunteers who preferred their left...	% of right-handed volunteers who showed no preference	% of left-handed volunteers who preferred their left...	% of left-handed volunteers who preferred their right...	% of left-handed volunteers who showed no preference
Foot						
Eye						
Ear						

people show a link between their dominant hand and their dominant foot, ear, and eye, and left-handed people don't.

● Cool lefty facts:

▸ Males are more likely to be left-handed than females.

▸ There is a higher proportion of left-ies among professional chess players, math teachers, architects, engineers, artists, astronauts, and musicians than in the general population.

▸ Lefties are more likely to have reading disabilities, migraine headaches, stuttering problems, and allergies.

▸ If both parents are right-handed, there's a 10 percent chance they will have a lefty child. If one parent is left-handed, their chances go up to 20 percent. And, if both parents are left-handed, there's a 26 percent chance they'll have a lefty offspring.

▸ If one identical twin is left-handed, then there's a 75 percent chance that the other twin will also be left-handed. Now, if handedness was totally genetic (hereditary), identical twins would always be both left-handed or right-handed.

● If you're a lefty, you may be in the minority, but you're in very good company. Here's a list of some famous (and infamous) lefties:

▸ Alexander the Great, military genius
▸ Napoleon Bonaparte, French emperor
▸ Boston Strangler, serial killer
▸ Julius Caesar, Roman general
▸ Fidel Castro, Cuban leader
▸ Charlie Chaplin, silent-movie actor
▸ Charlemagne, Roman emperor
▸ Bill Clinton, U.S. President
▸ Kurt Cobain, musician
▸ Phil Collins, musician
▸ Tom Cruise, actor
▸ Leonardo da Vinci, painter, inventor
▸ John Dillinger, bank robber
▸ Albert Einstein, physicist
▸ Queen Elizabeth of England
▸ M.C. Escher, painter
▸ Henry Ford, car manufacturer
▸ Benjamin Franklin, U.S. statesman
▸ Judy Garland, singer/actor
▸ King George II of England
▸ King George VI of England
▸ Dorothy Hamill, ice skater

▸ Jack-the-Ripper, serial killer
▸ Jimi Hendrix, musician
▸ Jim Henson, puppeteer
▸ Joan of Arc, French heroine
▸ Helen Keller, advocate for the blind
▸ King Louis XVI of France
▸ Paul McCartney, musician
▸ Michelangelo, sculptor/painter
▸ Marilyn Monroe, actor
▸ Pablo Picasso, painter
▸ Ronald Reagan, U.S. President
▸ Keanu Reeves, actor
▸ Julia Roberts, actor
▸ Babe Ruth, baseball player
▸ Jerry Seinfeld, comedian
▸ Harry S. Truman, U.S. President
▸ Mark Twain, novelist
▸ Queen Victoria of England
▸ H.G. Wells, author
▸ Bruce Willis, actor
▸ Oprah Winfrey, talk-show host

WHAT ELSE YOU CAN DO

● If you live in a neighborhood with a lot of pets, test the "handedness" of dogs, cats, or other animals.

The Grass Is Greener...

Check out your neighbors' lawns. Why is it that some lawns are so lush and green while others are scraggly and wilted? A lot depends on how the lawn is maintained. In many cases, that beautiful, healthy lawn is due to the use of chemical fertilizers that may not be healthy for the environment. Some prefer natural fertilizers that don't do as much harm, but do they work as well as chemical fertilizers?

PROBLEM/PURPOSE

What's the difference in grass growth when chemical or natural fertilizers are used?

EXPERIMENT SUMMARY

You'll grow several pots of grass to determine which fertilizer works better.

WHAT YOU NEED

► **12 pots**
► **Potting soil (make sure there are no chemicals added to the soil)**
► **2 different kinds of grass seeds (tall fescue and fine fescue, for example)**
► **Chemical fertilizer of your choice**
► **Organic fertilizer (composted material, manure, etc.)**
► **Water**
► **Ruler**

EXPERIMENTAL PROCEDURE

1. Fill each pot with the same amount of soil.

2. Measure out six equal amounts of the first type of grass. Then measure the same amount for the second type of grass.

3. Sprinkle the grass seed amounts into each of the pots. Use the masking tape and marker to label which grass is in each pot. At this time, decide which two pots of each type of grass will receive the chemical fertilizer, which two will receive the natural fertilizer, and which two will receive no fertilizer. Label them immediately. You'll end up with two pots of each type of grass and fertilizer (you can do more if you wish).

4. Add the proper amount of chemical fertilizer (according to the instructions on the label) to the

labeled pots. Add the organic fertilizer to the labeled pots. Don't fertilize the final four pots.

5. Place the pots in the same sunny location, and water them with the same amount of water every other day. Add fertilizer every other week.

CONCLUSION

Record which grass sprouts first. As the grass grows, record the length of the grass in each of the pots at least once a week with the ruler. Do this for each of the types of grass you're testing. Also observe and record which pots come in fuller. If you can, measure between the grass sprouts. Record your observations for at least two months. Don't just compare the two different fertilizers, but also compare the fertilized pots to the unfertilized pots. Did both kinds of fertilizer do better than the unfertilized pots? What's your advice to your neighbors about how to keep their lawns looking green and mean?

TAKE A CLOSER LOOK

● There's no doubt that chemical fertilizers are easy to use; they contain nitrogen, phosphorous, and potassium—chemicals that all plants need. Nitrogen gives the leafy parts of plants more color and fresh growth. When there's not enough nitrogen in your grass, the lawn will look pale yellow. Phosphorous helps grass improve root growth, which gives it a firmer stand in the soil. Potassium helps keep grass healthy and helps it withstand disease. Sounds wonderful, right? Well, one problem is that many people use fertilizer whether

their grass needs it or not. Too much of one nutrient can damage plants. Plus, since chemical fertilizers are soluble, or easily dissolved, they're immediately available to plants (which is great), though only for a short period of time, since they quickly leach away and end up in groundwater or runoff, polluting water sources (not so great). Organic matter, though not helpful for a plant's growth until it decomposes, lasts a long time. Also, unlike chemical fertilizers, organic matter improves the water-holding capacity of soil, adds materials back into the soil that microorganisms break down into a form the plants can use, and suppresses certain plant diseases.

● These are the essential nutrients plants need to grow: carbon, oxygen, hydrogen, nitrogen, phosphorus, potassium, iron, zinc, sulfur, boron, calcium, magnesium, manganese, copper, chlorine, and molybdenum.

DISPLAY TIPS

● Bring a few of your grass pots to the fair. Also, research the ingredients in chemical fertilizers, and note the different environmental hazards that they pose. Post your findings on your display board.

Caffeinated Typing

You've probably observed family and friends starting their day with a cup of coffee or tea, or a can of soda. They may claim it helps them wake up. "Hmm," you may have said, "what physical effects does caffeine really have on the body?" If you've ever asked that question, this experiment's for you.

PROBLEM/PURPOSE

What effect does caffeine have on a person's typing speed?

EXPERIMENT SUMMARY

You'll test the typing speed (words per minute) of 20 volunteers. Then, 10 will drink caffeinated colas while the other 10 will drink decaffeinated colas. Their typing speeds will be tested again and compared.

WHAT YOU NEED

- ▶ **2 typing tests**
- ▶ **20 people, the same age: 10 girls, 10 boys**
- ▶ **Computer with printer**
- ▶ **Stopwatch**
- ▶ **Diet cola with caffeine***
- ▶ **Diet cola without caffeine***

* Note: Use diet sodas to avoid sugar, which might have other effects on your test participants.

EXPERIMENTAL PROCEDURE

1. To devise the typing test, you need to make sure each test is of equal difficulty. One easy way to do this is to choose two different pages from the same book.

2. Find 20 volunteers for the experiment. Preferably, choose volunteers who don't drink a lot of coffee or colas regularly.

3. If you only have one computer, you'll have to test your volunteers one at a time. To make your experiment less time consuming, ask your school if you can borrow the computer lab. Just make sure nobody's drinking cola in the lab!

4. Ask your first volunteer to sit down at the computer, and explain to them that they will start typing the page in front of them as soon as you say "start." Tell them not to go back and correct misspellings or punctuation—just keep typing. Tell him to stop when you say "stop."

5. Set your timer for two minutes and begin the test. Stop the typing when time has run out.

How much caffeine do you ingest a day?

Product	Milligrams of Caffeine
Coffee (8 oz [240 mL])	65 to 120
Decaffeinated coffee (8 oz [240 mL])	2 to 4
Cola (8 oz [240 mL])	20 to 40
Chocolate milk (8 oz [240 mL])	2 to 7
Brewed tea (8 ounces [240 mL])	20 to 90
Milk chocolate (1 oz [28 g])	1 to 15
Dark chocolate, semi-sweet (1 oz [28 g])	5 to 40

6. Have the volunteer drink 16 ounces (480 mL) of diet cola (10 of your volunteers will drink caffeinated cola while the other 10 will drink decaffeinated cola). Record in your journal whether the volunteer is drinking caffeinated or decaffeinated cola. Make sure the volunteer doesn't know which he or she is drinking.

7. Wait 30 minutes and then have the volunteer once again sit down at the computer.

8. Use the second typing test (or another page of the same book), and time the volunteer for two minutes.

9. Repeat with the other volunteers. Keep in mind that half of your volunteers will be drinking decaffeinated cola.

10. Once the volunteers are finished, record in your notebook the numbers of words typed before and after drinking the cola. Note the difference in the number of words of those who drank the caffeinated cola. Then, note the difference in the number of words of those who drank the decaffeinated cola.

11. Compute the average difference between the two tests among the caffeinated and decaffeinated groups, and then compare the differences.

CONCLUSION

What differences, if any, did you discover between the two test groups? Did the caffeinated group type more, less, or the same as before they drank the caffeine? And how did their numbers compare to the decaffeinated group? Did you notice any other changes in your test subjects—did they seem more alert? Also, how did the caffeine affect accuracy? Were there more or fewer mistakes in the test group after drinking caffeine?

TAKE A CLOSER LOOK

● Caffeine is a naturally occurring substance found in the leaves, seeds, and fruits of over 50 different plant species. The most commonly known sources of caffeine are coffee and cocoa beans, tea leaves, and kola nuts.

● Those who say caffeine helps them wake up in the morning may be telling the truth: caffeine acts as a mild stimulant to the central nervous system, perhaps making us feel more "awake." But the effects of caffeine usually wear off after a few hours, and the more caffeine you drink, the more you'll need for it to affect you.

● Studies have also shown that caffeine may increase memory and improve reasoning powers.

● On the average, adults ingest 200 mg of caffeine a day, while children intake less than 40 mg a day. Adults get most of their caffeine from coffee, while kids get theirs from soft drinks, tea, and in some cases, chocolate.

The Sound of Music

Do you have a favorite song you like to listen to when you're in a bad mood? Or does your sports team listen to a certain kind of music to get pumped up for a big game? It's clear that music can affect our lives, but how?

PROBLEM/PURPOSE

How do different kinds of music affect heart rate?

EXPERIMENT SUMMARY

You'll gather a selection of different kinds of music to play for your volunteers, and then check heart rates to see if the music you're playing for them is either making their hearts beat slower or faster.

WHAT YOU NEED

▶ **10 volunteers, 5 boys, 5 girls, the same age**
▶ **Comfortable chair**
▶ **Heart-rate monitor (optional)**
▶ **Stopwatch**
▶ **CD or tape player**
▶ **Headphones**
▶ **1 hard rock/heavy metal song***
▶ **1 rap song***
▶ **1 classical song***
▶ **1 rhythm and blues song***

* Each song should be at least three minutes long.

EXPERIMENTAL PROCEDURE

1. Ask your volunteers to refrain from exercising vigorously or eating for one hour before the experiment.

2. Ask the first volunteer to sit in the comfortable chair and relax. Lower the lights, and let the volunteer sit in the chair for up to 15 minutes. This is to ensure that the volunteer is relaxed in order to obtain a resting heart rate.

3. Take the volunteer's pulse. If you're using a heart-rate monitor, simply read the display and record the rate. If you're manually taking the pulse, take your thumb and place it on one inner arm near the wrist. Don't press too hard—you might end up feeling the blood in your own fingers. Keep your stopwatch where you can see it, and count how many beats you feel in a 10-second period. Multiply the result by 6 and that's the resting heart rate. Record it in your note-

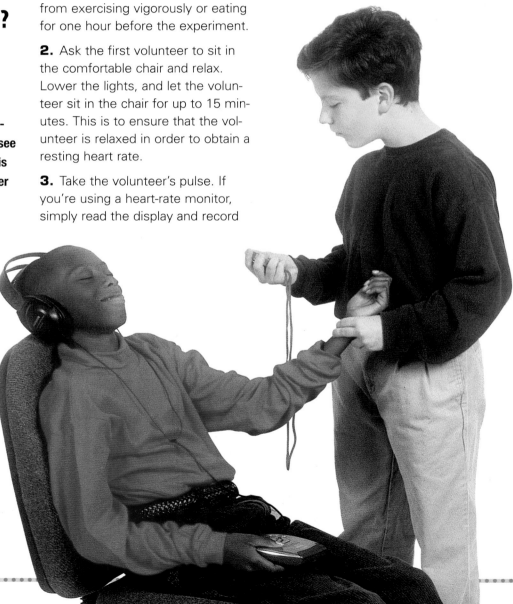

book under the heading "No Music: Resting Heart Rate."

4. Place the headphones over the volunteer's ears, and play the first song you selected. Make sure the volume is comfortable and the same for all the songs.

5. Take the volunteer's pulse twice during the song: halfway through the song and right after the song ends. Record the two heart rates in your notebook.

6. Let the volunteer relax for three minutes, or until his/her pulse returns to the resting heart rate you recorded before playing the first song.

7. Repeat steps 4 through 6 for the rest of the songs.

8. Repeat the whole experiment with the rest of your volunteers.

9. Find the average heart rate of the volunteers during each song. This is the number you use to compare to the resting heart rate to discover if there was a change in heart rate.

10. Find the average of the volunteers' resting heart rates, and compare it to the average of the heart rates for each of the different kinds of music used in the test. This is your data for the conclusion.

CONCLUSION

After examining the results, can you conclude that one type of music caused pulse rates to increase more

than others? Or did the pulse rates stay the same under different types of music? Was there a difference between boys and girls? What qualities in the music do you think caused pulse rates to be faster? Did any type of music cause the pulse rates to be slower? If a group of teenagers are warming up for a game, which kind of music would be best to play? What type of music would you recommend for a hospital where people need to stay calm and relaxed?

TAKE A CLOSER LOOK

● Listening to music has been shown to affect mood, reduce pain, decrease blood pressure, reduce anxiety, improve motor functioning, improve respiration and vital capacity (see page 60), and more.

● Your heart beats about 40 million times a year, circulating 4,000 gallons (15,200 L) of blood a day.

● The average person has a resting heart rate between 70 and 80 beats a minute, whereas an Olympic athlete's pulse may be as low as 50.

WHAT ELSE YOU CAN DO

● Spend some time in a fast-food restaurant and listen to the music they play. Does the music affect how the patrons eat? Some restaurants have actually done research that shows that we eat to the beat. So, if we actually eat according to the speed of the music being played, what should the restaurant do if it's really busy?

● Instead of music, test the difference in heart rates while your subjects play different video games.

● If music affects people's lives, what is music's effect on plant growth?

DISPLAY TIPS

A photograph of your testing location will give the judges a good sense of how well you tried to control your variables. A dark room with very few distractions will show the judges you know what you're doing. Also, display the CDs or tapes you played.

Memories

When you're introduced to someone, do you remember his or her name, or do you usually forget it pretty quickly? How about phone numbers? Do you forget phone numbers people give you? Remembering things like names, numbers, and lists is a function of what's called *working memory*. With this experiment, you'll try to see if there is a difference between the working memories of boys and girls.

PROBLEM/PURPOSE

How does gender affect working memory?

EXPERIMENT SUMMARY

You'll gather a series of images for your volunteers to look at and try to memorize. Then they'll have to recall as many of the images as possible.

WHAT YOU NEED

▶ **12 to 15 magazine images (car, flowers, etc.)**
▶ **Glue**
▶ **Poster board**
▶ **15 male volunteers, same age**
▶ **15 female volunteers, same age**
▶ **Watch**

EXPERIMENTAL PROCEDURE

1. Cut out 12 to 15 easily identifiable pictures from magazines. Paste the pictures on the poster board equal distances apart.

2. Tell the first volunteer that you'll show him/her a poster board with

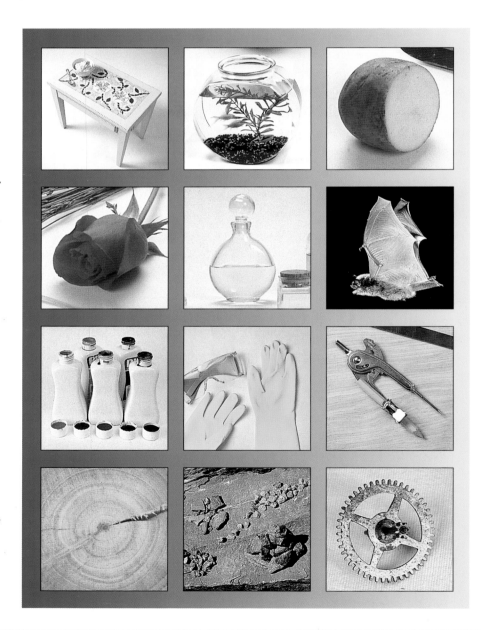

various images on it, and they're to memorize as many of the images as they can in one minute.

3. Show the poster board to the first volunteer for exactly one minute, then turn the board over.

4. Have the volunteer write down as many images as he/she can recall. Give the volunteer 45 seconds. Record how many pictures he/she recalled.

5. Repeat steps 2 through 4 for the rest of the volunteers.

6. Average the number of correctly recalled images of the girls and the boys, and compare.

CONCLUSION

Was there a difference between girls' and boys' working memories? Show your results in a bar graph or pie chart. How do your results compare to your research? Finally, ask your volunteers how they memorized the pictures. Was there one method that a majority of the volunteers used? Was there a method that worked best?

WHAT ELSE YOU CAN DO

● Do the first part of the experiment, then teach your volunteers one or more of the memory tricks in the Take a Closer Look section, and retest. Did the volunteers remember more than before learning the memory trick?

● Why are phone numbers seven digits? Test the limits of working

memory! Show your volunteers a series of three random letters for five seconds and then have them write down the letters they saw. Then show the volunteers four different random letters. Then five, six, seven...keep showing them increasing numbers of random letters until they can't recall them all. Record how many letters the volunteers recall before their memories fail them.

TAKE A CLOSER LOOK

● Long-term memory retains information from the past: where you went on vacation five years ago, the color of your shoes in first grade, what you had for dinner the other night. Working memory, on the other hand, stores recently learned information for a short period of time, and allows us to use and eventually store that information. But the information in our working memories can be quickly forgotten. For example, you look up a phone number in the phone directory. You get the number and close the book. As you walk over to the phone you're saying the number over and over in your head (a great way to keep information in your working memory), and then your sister asks you a question. Guess what? The number's gone, and you have to look it up again. Rehearsing the information in your working memory is not the only way to remember it. In fact, there are a variety of strategies that can be used to train the brain to hold more

information in its working memory. These strategies are called *mnemonic* (pronounced: ni-mon-ik; from the Greek word meaning "mind") devices, and they're great for taking tests that ask you to memorize lots of names, dates, and lists. Here are just a few mnemonic devices:

VISUALIZATION

You'll have a better chance of remembering something if you make up an absurd image to go with it. For example, say you have to buy eggs, bread, milk, and cookies at the store. If you don't want to write a list, you can create an absurd situation like: the eggs fell off my head, spilled my milk, which soaked my bread and cookie sandwich.

CHUNKING

Remembering things in small pieces is easier than remembering the whole. That's why phone numbers and other long numbers that are necessary to remember have spaces or dashes between them.

ACROSTICS

An *acrostic* is a phrase that uses the first letter of words to remember them. An old favorite is "Roy G. Biv," which is an acrostic for the colors in a rainbow: **R**ed, **O**range, **Y**ellow, **G**reen, **B**lue, **I**ndigo, **V**iolet. Here's one for the planets: **M**y **V**ery **E**ducated **M**other **J**ust **S**howed **U**s **N**ine **P**lanets.

Color Confusion

Imagine opening a bottle of fizzy red root beer or pouring a glass of orange juice that flowed creamy white. What flavor would you expect when you took your first sip? Do people associate certain flavors with particular colors?

PROBLEM/PURPOSE

How does color affect taste?

EXPERIMENT SUMMARY

In this taste test, you'll analyze your volunteers' ability to correctly indicate the flavors they're tasting, even if the color is wrong.

WHAT YOU NEED

- ▶ **12 clear plastic cups**
- ▶ **Water**
- ▶ **Measuring spoons**
- ▶ **Sugar**
- ▶ **Red, yellow, and green food colorings**
- ▶ **Masking tape**
- ▶ **Permanent marker**
- ▶ **Strawberry, orange, peppermint, and pineapple extracts**
- ▶ **At least 10 taste testers**
- ▶ **Crackers**

EXPERIMENTAL PROCEDURE

1. Fill the 12 cups with ½ cup (120 mL) of water, and add 1 tablespoon (14 g) of sugar to each. Stir until the sugar dissolves in each cup.

2. Add the food coloring to the cups to make three glasses of each color: red, yellow, green, and orange (mix red and yellow). Number each of the cups 1 through 12 with the masking tape and marker. Number the cups so that each group of four will contain each of the colors.

3. For cups 1 through 4, don't add anything to the colored sugar water.

4. For cups 5 through 8, add the pineapple, peppermint, orange, and strawberry extracts so that they don't match the colors in the cups (don't put strawberry extract into red sugar water, or orange into orange, etc.).

5. For cups 9 through 12, add the extracts to their matching colors (orange in orange, yellow in pineapple, peppermint in green, and strawberry in red).

6. Record in your notebook the cups that are flavored and the ones that aren't.

7. Have your first volunteer taste each of the liquids in cups 1 through 4 and tell what flavor they're tasting. Remember, at this point they're only tasting sugar water.

8. Have the volunteer eat a cracker, and then repeat the process with cups 5 through 8. Record the color of each drink, the actual flavor, and the flavor your subject believes it is. At this point, your volunteer is drinking extracts with the wrong colors.

9. Have the volunteer eat another cracker, and then repeat the process with cups 9 through 12. Record the color of each drink, the actual flavor, and the flavor your subject believes it is. Your volunteer is drinking extracts with the correct colors.

10. Repeat steps 1 through 9 with at least 9 other people.

CONCLUSION

Make sure your volunteers drink the colored sugar water first, the mixed-up extracts second, and the correct extract/color last. Note the success/failure rate of each of the volunteers' attempts with each cup. Were the volunteers fooled by the plain sugar water? Did they think the green sugar water tasted like mint or the yellow like pineapple? Or did they pick something else? Were the volunteers successful at going beyond color in indicating that cups 5 through 8 tasted differently than the colors would have indicated? Finally, if your volunteers couldn't tell what flavor cups 9 through 12 were, then your experiment will not be valid. You may need to add more extract to cups 5 through 12. Also, pay particular attention to the cups in which everyone guessed incorrectly. Double-check your cups and flavors before reaching any conclusions.

TAKE A CLOSER LOOK

● You've got about 10,000 taste buds, which are located primarily in four different parts of your tongue. Each location is supposedly good at tasting something specific. The next time you eat something sweet, salty, bitter, or sour, pay attention to where on your tongue you're tasting it. Also, if something is too sweet, salty, bitter, or sour, and you don't want to spit it out, find the place on your tongue where you won't taste it as much. Can you pinpoint locations on your tongue that are better at tasting different flavors than other locations? Though often regarded as fact, many scientists now question whether or not the tongue has sweet, salty, bitter, and sour spots. What do you think?

DISPLAY TIPS

● Walking around the science fair is guaranteed to make some judges and guests a bit thirsty, and they'll probably welcome a chance to guess at a sample of flavored water. Mix up a pitcher of water and food coloring. Add a flavor that doesn't match the color of the water (i.e., pineapple flavor and red coloring). Set the pitcher out on a corner of your display table with a stack of plastic cups so that the judges and guests can sample for themselves. Write the name of the flavor on an index card and tape it facedown in front of the pitcher. On top of the card instruct them to take a sample drink and guess the flavor they taste, then lift the card to find out the real flavor.

The Great Cricket Burglar Alarm Experiment

Sure, dogs and cats make great pets, but did you know that in many Asian cultures crickets are often the pet of choice? And why not? You don't have to walk them, feeding them doesn't cost much, and they don't ruin the furniture. And if you're thinking that your dog is the better choice because it keeps the crooks away, crickets may actually also help keep your house safe from unwanted visitors.

PROBLEM/PURPOSE

How will the introduction of an unfamiliar person to a cricket's adopted home affect the cricket's chirping rate?

EXPERIMENT SUMMARY

You'll keep a cricket as a pet, and once the cricket is familiar with the family, it'll continue to chirp when family members enter and leave a room. You'll test what effect an unfamiliar person will have on the cricket's chirping rate.

WHAT YOU NEED

▶ **Cricket**

▶ **Large glass jar (or a small aquarium with a tight-fitting lid)**

▶ **Cheesecloth**

▶ **Rubber band**

▶ **Use of a room in your house that gets a lot of traffic (living room, den, etc.)**

▶ **Use of your family**

▶ **5 volunteers**

EXPERIMENTAL PROCEDURE

1. Get permission from your parents before beginning your experiment. They may not be too happy about the chirping.

2. Catch a male cricket. If you're having trouble finding one outdoors, you can purchase crickets at pet supply stores (crickets make great reptile food). Ask for either a house cricket or a field cricket. It's pretty easy to tell the females from the males. Male crickets are the ones that sing. But you can also tell the difference between males and females by the female's long "tail," which is used for laying eggs (called the *ovipositor*).

3. Place the cricket in the jar, and place a piece of the cheesecloth over the mouth of the jar. Use the

rubber band to secure the cheese-cloth.

4. Place the jar in the living room or den of your home. Care for your cricket (see Take a Closer Look), and wait until the cricket starts chirping even when members of the family come and go from the room. That means the cricket is used to you. Also record when your cricket is most likely to chirp so you can have your volunteers come to your house at a good time (crickets sing mostly at night).

5. To test how familiar the cricket is with your family, wait until the cricket is chirping, and have your family enter the room one at a time. If the cricket doesn't stop chirping, you're ready to proceed with the experiment.

6. Wait until your cricket is chirping, and have one family member enter the room and approach the cricket. Record what your cricket does. After one minute, have the family member leave. Repeat with the rest of the family members.

7. Repeat the same process with the volunteers. Record what the cricket does after each volunteer enters the room. Make sure the cricket starts chirping again before sending the next volunteer into the room.

CONCLUSION

Record your cricket's success rate. Did it stop chirping with each of the volunteers? How close to the jar did the volunteers have to go before it stopped chirping?

TAKE A CLOSER LOOK

● When doing this experiment, make sure you're only using one cricket. Male crickets are very territorial and will try to kill another one in the same jar. Male crickets will live up to two months if properly cared for.

● Male crickets sing to attract the females and to scare off the competition from other males.

● To make your cricket feel more comfortable in its new home, spread some sand on the bottom of the jar. A rock will give the cricket a place to hide, and some leaves may make the cricket feel a little more at home. Experiment with little pieces of food to see what your cricket prefers. Try small pieces of apple, lettuce, potato, carrot, and other fruits and vegetables. Also try bread crumbs. Take out any food the cricket won't eat. Spray a little water in the jar or aquarium.

● Crickets chirp by rubbing their wings together. A vein on one wing makes the sound louder as the other wing rubs against it. Since crickets are cold-blooded, as the temperature rises, their metabolism speeds up, which means they chirp faster when it gets warmer. Some say you can even estimate the temperature (Fahrenheit) by counting the chirps in 15 seconds and adding 40. For Celsius, count the number of chirps in 7 seconds and add 5 to get the temperature. Try it out!

WHAT ELSE YOU CAN DO

● You can test whether or not different types of music affect the rate of a cricket's chirping.

● Experiment how environmental factors, such as light and temperature affect a cricket's chirping.

> **"**If I could change anything about my project, I would have typed everything for my display, instead of writing it all. Typing would have made it look much neater."
> —Holly Aldridge, 7th grader

The Balance of Nature

Imagine that you're trapped inside a jar with only the basics you need for survival: air, water, and food (okay, we'll throw in a book to keep you from getting bored). Eventually you'd use up all of these basics, and at the same time, find yourself trapped in your own waste. Yuck! But, with the proper mixture of plants and other organisms to keep you company, you'd most likely survive in a balance of nature.

PROBLEM/PURPOSE

How do different proportions of plants and animals affect the overall health of a closed system?

EXPERIMENT SUMMARY

You'll set up three terrariums with different proportions of plants and snails to see which arrangement produces the best conditions for maintaining the lives of all of the organisms.

WHAT YOU NEED

- ▶ **6 jars with lids, 1 quart (.95 L)**
- ▶ **Masking tape**
- ▶ **Permanent marker**
- ▶ **Purified water**
- ▶ **8 freshwater snails***
- ▶ **8 aquarium plants***
- ▶ **Aquarium sand**
- ▶ **pH test kit**
- ▶ **Dissolved oxygen test kit**
- ▶ **Thermometer**

* Consult with the aquarium staff at a pet store to select the best varieties for your trials.

EXPERIMENTAL PROCEDURE

1. Label the jars 1 through 6, and fill the bottom of each jar with 1 inch (2.5 cm) of sand.

2. Fill each jar with the purified water, leaving 1 inch (2.5 cm) of air space between the water and the top of the jar.

3. Place a thermometer inside each jar so that you can read it.

4. Place two aquarium plants in each of the jars labeled 1,2, 3, and 4. Make sure the plant roots are buried in the sand.

5. Place two snails in each of the jars labeled 3, 4, 5, and 6.

6. Screw the lids tightly onto each of the jars, and set them together in a safe place in your house. They shouldn't be put in direct sunlight, and should be kept at room temperature.

7. Record the date and time of day in your journal, and also write a description of the general conditions of the plants, snails, and water in the jars.

8. Once each day for 14 days, observe the color of the plants, the health of the snails, the water clarity, temperature, pH, and dissolved oxygen levels. Come up with a number scale with explanations for judging the water clarity and color (for example, 0 = mud-colored, 1 = coffee-colored, 2 = black tea-colored, 3 = apple juice-colored, 4 = lemonade-colored, 5 = clear water).

CONCLUSION

Which jar supported life the longest? How did the jar with just plants compare with the jar that only had snails? Which jar had the greatest change in water conditions? Which jar had the greatest pH change? What about dissolved oxygen? Was the water temperature constant in all of the jars, or did it differ between the jars? If you were a snail, which jar would you want to live in for the healthiest conditions? What if you were a

plant? Your display will benefit from graphs of all of these factors from the 14 days of observations.

TAKE A CLOSER LOOK

● The snails in your jars are dependent on the plants to absorb carbon dioxide and produce oxygen in the closed system. When there are too many plants and not enough snails, there's not enough carbon dioxide in the jars to support the plants' needs. When there are too many snails and not enough plants, the snails use up the oxygen faster than the plants can produce it. Furthermore, the process of decay following the death of the plants or snails requires oxygen, and that'll add carbon dioxide to the system. When the system becomes unbalanced and waste materials build up, the water loses clarity, and the pH may change. When the right balance is achieved, both organisms have the nutrients they need for survival, and the conditions in the jar stay fairly constant.

● Earth is like a giant jar filled with plants and animals and a variety of other organisms interacting with each other and the nonliving environment for survival. When there's too much of one thing or not enough of another, the effects spread throughout the unbalanced system. You've probably heard a lot about the destruction of the world's forests, from stands of old growth in British Columbia to tropical rainforests in South America. The loss of forests around the world is a concern to scientists and environmentalists for many reasons, including the role forests play as the "lungs of the planet"—converting carbon dioxide in the air (the stuff we exhale and produce from burning fossil fuels and wood) into the oxygen animals like ourselves need to survive. The loss of the world's forests means there are fewer plants to help convert carbon dioxide (a major greenhouse gas) to oxygen, and worse, the burning of these forests adds even more carbon dioxide to the atmosphere. An increase in the amount of greenhouse gases in the atmosphere (gases which trap sunlight around the earth) is thought to contribute to rising global temperatures, or global warming. Trees and plants are also essential players in Earth's water and soil cycles, and the destruction of huge tracts of forest may affect weather systems and change local climates—creating deserts where there was once lush, forested mountain slopes.

Bacteria Wars

The world needs bacteria to survive; however, too much bacteria, or the wrong type of bacteria, can lead to many different kinds of diseases. There are many different household cleaners available in the fight against the spread of bacteria. Which one works best?

PROBLEM/PURPOSE

Which household cleaner will kill bacteria best?

EXPERIMENT SUMMARY

Using four different household cleaners that claim to kill bacteria and an area contaminated with bacteria, you'll determine which cleaner works best.

WHAT YOU NEED

- **Masking tape**
- **Permanent marker**
- **8 sterile petri dishes***
- **Saucepan**
- **Measuring cup**
- **1 cup (.24 L) distilled water**
- **Measuring spoons**
- **1 tablespoon (14 g) unflavored gelatin**
- **1 beef bouillon cube**
- **Spoon (to dissolve mixture)**
- **Kitchen counter**
- **2 eggs**
- **Fork**
- **Bowl**
- **9 pairs of latex gloves**
- **Basting brush**
- **8 sterile gauze pads**
- **1 box of sterile cotton swabs**
- **4 liquid cleansers (name brands up to you)**
- **A warm, dark location**

* Petri dishes are available at science supply stores and in many stores that sell school supplies (ask your teacher if you're having trouble finding them).

EXPERIMENTAL PROCEDURE

1. Label the *bottom* of each petri dish 1 through 8, since the tops can get mixed up.

2. Before you do anything else, you have to make some yummy bacteria food. Like all living things, bacteria need food to thrive. Here's a nifty recipe that will make the bacteria cry for seconds.

3. Add 1 cup (.24 L) of distilled water to a saucepan. Bring to a boil, and add the gelatin and one beef bouillon cube to the water.

4. Stir constantly until the gelatin and cube dissolve completely.

5. Carefully pour the hot mix into each petri dish until half full. Place the lids over the dishes immediately. Wait until the gelatin sets before continuing.

6. Section off a countertop into four small equal sections with masking tape. Number each section with the tape. At this time, assign two petri dishes for each section, and record the numbers in your notebook.

7. Crack open the eggs into the bowl. Mix the eggs with the fork. Let the mixed egg sit for one hour at room temperature.

8. Put on a pair of gloves, and with the brush, wipe the egg onto each sectioned-off piece of countertop. Throw away the gloves.

9. Put on a new pair of gloves, and with one of the sterile swabs, take a smear of section 1 and gently glide it across its corresponding petri dish. Close the lid immediately. Throw away the gloves. Repeat this procedure for each section. Note: Be careful not to touch the prepared petri dishes with your hands. The bacteria on your hands would be happy to enjoy the bacteria food you've prepared. So, wear the gloves!

10. Using a sterile gauze pad, clean section 1 with one of the four cleansers. Repeat with the other three sections. Make sure to use a different cleanser and gauze pad for each section, and change gloves after each cleaning.

11. After each section is cleaned, take a smear of that section of countertop with separate swabs and gently glide the swabs over the second set of corresponding petri dishes. Close each lid immediately. The first set of petri dishes acts as your control group. The experimental group is your second set.

12. After all the dishes have been smeared and sealed, place them in a dark, warm area of your home. Closets, small rooms, and warm basements work well. Then wash your hands and the countertop with hot, soapy water.

13. Check the dishes for bacterial growth every 12 hours for 5 days.

Record any changes in the dishes. Note the color, size, and shape of the bacteria, and the differences between the control and experimental dishes. Whatever you do, don't open the lids. Photograph the dishes for your presentation.

14. After five days, record your results. After all data has been recorded, throw away the dishes.

CONCLUSION

Look at your control dishes first. Are there any differences between them? If so, you really can't make a valid comparison between the cleansers. You'll only be able to compare the experimental dish to its corresponding control dish. This

means that different amounts of bacteria were added to each dish. If, however, your control dishes look similar, you can compare bacterial growth between the different cleansers. Be as descriptive as possible with your observations. Use a table to note your observations for each time you checked for growth. Also, when describing the bacteria growth in the dishes, remember that you'll be describing *colonies* of bacteria and not the individual bacterium, since a single bacterium is too small to be seen without a microscope.

TAKE A CLOSER LOOK

● This experiment only tests which cleansers kill bacteria that like gelatin and beef food best. Some bacteria prefer milk, sugar, or soy foods. Your teacher may be able to help you get these materials.

● It is estimated that up to one third of the world's population suffers from food poisoning every year. Harmful microorganisms or bacteria that can't be seen without a microscope cause this problem. Harmful bacteria grow readily in foods at room temperature, especially meat, fish, and dairy products.

WHAT ELSE YOU CAN DO

● You can perform experiments like this with all sorts of household products. Watch the advertisements on television for inspiration.

Family Fingerprints

Look closely at the ridges, whorls, and lines that dominate the surface of your fingertips. Those markings are unique to you. Your fingerprint is your personal identification code, and it's one of the easiest ways for police departments around the world to trace and identify criminals. In fact, the U.S. Federal Bureau of Investigation has more than 34 million fingerprint cards stored in its archives—enough, they say, to make 18 stacks of cards each as tall as a skyscraper! A closer look at the characteristics of your fingerprints may even tell where you come from.

PROBLEM/PURPOSE

What effect does heredity have on fingerprint characteristics?

EXPERIMENT SUMMARY

You'll try to match children to their parents by the characteristics of their fingerprints.

WHAT YOU NEED

- ▶ **Four families (specifically parents and their children)**
- ▶ **Index cards**
- ▶ **Black ink pad or fingerprint kit**
- ▶ **Magnifying glass**
- ▶ **Hand wipes**
- ▶ **Fingerprint chart (see page 59)**

EXPERIMENTAL PROCEDURE

1. All the participants must wash their hands and dry them thoroughly.

2. Practice taking fingerprints until you can make a print that's clear.

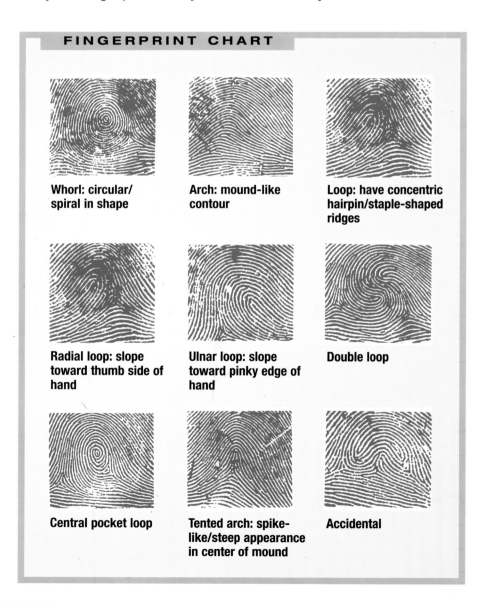

FINGERPRINT CHART

Whorl: circular/spiral in shape

Arch: mound-like contour

Loop: have concentric hairpin/staple-shaped ridges

Radial loop: slope toward thumb side of hand

Ulnar loop: slope toward pinky edge of hand

Double loop

Central pocket loop

Tented arch: spike-like/steep appearance in center of mound

Accidental

	Card 1: thumb	Card 2: thumb	Card 3: thumb	Card 4: thumb	Card 5: thumb	Card 6: thumb	Card 7: thumb
Whorl	✓			✓			
Arch			✓				
Loop		✓					
Radial Loop					✓		✓
Ulnar Loop						✓	

3. Assign each person a number, and write this number on the back of the index card you're going to use for their fingerprints. Make a list in your journal with each person's name and number for reference later.

4. For each person, make a print of each of the fingers on their right hand (including the thumb) on the side of their index card that's not numbered. Repeat this with each family.

5. Mix up all of the fingerprint cards and stack them numbered side down.

6. Select a card and compare the characteristics with the fingerprint chart on page 59. Identify the primary trait of each finger, and write it next to the print. For example, if you identify a radial loop on the thumb, then write "radial loop" below the thumbprint; if you identify a mound on the index finger, write "mound" below the index fingerprint. Analyze each of the cards in the stack this way. If you notice other common characteristics, note them on the card as well.

7. Sort the cards so that those with similar patterns are next to each other.

8. Check the numbers on the backs of the cards and cross-reference them with your names list. Write the names on the cards on the same side as the fingerprints.

CONCLUSION

After identifying the characteristics of each of the fingerprints, did you find that any of them shared similar traits? For example, did you find some thumbprints had whorls while others possessed arches? When you matched the numbers to the names list, did you find any relationship between the prints of family members? Do any of the children's fingerprints have traits like those of their parents, or do siblings have similar fingerprints? Check your analysis by having another person compare the fingerprint patterns for similarities. Teach him/her how to identify the fingerprints using the chart, and see if they agree with your analysis. Create five charts, one for each finger, and check off the characteristics you find, and then compare.

TAKE A CLOSER LOOK

● Sir Francis Galton and Sir Edward R. Henry came up with the system for analyzing and classifying fingerprints, which was introduced to British authorities at Scotland Yard in 1901. Essentially, the fingerprint is defined by the pattern made by the ridges on the tips of the fingers and thumb. As shown in the chart, there are specific characteristics of fingerprints that are analyzed for identification. Compare your fingerprints with the chart, and note the characteristics that appear in your print.

● *Dactyloscopy* is the technique of fingerprinting.

● Fingerprints were first used as a form of signature on contracts and ancient texts.

● Is it really true that no two fingerprints are exactly alike? Well, according to statistical calculations by Sir Francis Galton, an anthropologist who studied them in the 1800s, the odds of two people having the same fingerprints is approximately 1 in every 64 billion. At the present world population of 6 billion, it's probably safe to assume that your prints are indeed unique.

Where There's Secondhand Smoke...

Everybody knows that smoking isn't good for you, but what about inhaling other people's smoke? This experiment will measure one possible effect of secondhand smoke.

PROBLEM/PURPOSE

How does involuntary smoking (secondhand smoke) affect a kid's vital lung capacity?

EXPERIMENT
SUMMARY

Using a homemade *spirometer* (an instrument that measures the volume of air in the lungs), you'll compare the maximum volume of air the lungs can hold of kids whose parents smoke versus kids whose parents don't smoke.

WHAT YOU NEED

- ▶ **2-liter, clear-plastic cola bottle**
- ▶ **Ruler**
- ▶ **Permanent marker**
- ▶ **Water**
- ▶ **Large bowl**
- ▶ **A trustworthy helper**
- ▶ **Approximately 2 feet (.6 m) of rubber tubing**
- ▶ **20 volunteers***

* The volunteers all must be the same gender and age. Choose kids who aren't active in sports. Also, 10 volunteers need to have parents who smoke in their presence (in the home, the car, etc.), and the other 10 need to have parents who don't smoke.

EXPERIMENTAL PROCEDURE

1. To assemble the spirometer, you first need to devise a measuring system for the cola bottle. The best way to do this is to use the ruler to measure centimeter marks starting on the bottom of the bottle, and marking them with the marker all the way up the bottle. Number the first centimeter mark 1, the second 2, and so forth all the way up.

2. Add 3 to 4 inches (7.6 to 10.2 cm) of water in the bowl. Fill the bottle completely with water, and turn it upside down into the water in the bowl. Be careful not to let any air into the bottle.

3. Have your helper hold the bottle while you place one end of the tubing into the bottle.

4. Have your first volunteer inhale as deeply as he/she can and exhale

completely into the tubing. Record the measurement.

5. Repeat the test three more times, and average the four measurements for your final measurement.

6. Repeat for each of your volunteers. Average the capacities of the two groups: the kids with parents who smoke and the kids whose parents don't smoke. Compare the results to come up with your conclusion.

CONCLUSION

After comparing your results, what did you notice? Did secondhand smoke affect lung capacity at all? How do your results affect the way you feel about smoking in public places, such as restaurants?

TAKE A CLOSER LOOK

● When you inhale, air goes through your mouth or nose and goes down the windpipe, or *trachea*. On the way down, tiny hairs called *cilia* move gently to keep dirt out of the lungs. If you're a smoker (or exposed to cigarette smoke) the cilia become damaged and can no longer effectively keep the dirt out. Secretions build up in the airways, providing a place for infections to begin, clogging up airways even further. Now,

once the air gets past the windpipe, it travels through two large tubes that branch off into smaller tubes, or *bronchi*, that get smaller and smaller and smaller. The tiniest are called *bronchioles*, and each lung has around 30,000 of them. At the end of each bronchiole is a clump of air sacs called *alveoli* (there are over 600 million of them in your lungs!). Each of these has a covering of very tiny blood vessels called *capillaries*. The alveoli allow oxygen to pass through their walls into the capillaries, and then it's off to the heart. Cigarette smoke causes the walls of the alveoli to break down, making it much harder to breathe. Finally, if you need more proof that smoking shouldn't be the hobby of choice for anyone, cigarette smoke consists of 4,700 different chemicals, including over 200 known poisons and 40 cancer-causing substances, some of which are increased in secondhand smoke.

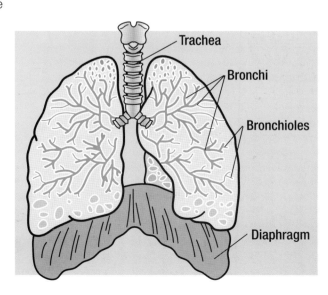

Paper or Plastic?

Many grocery stores offer a choice of bags: paper or plastic. Manufacturers of both say that their bags are better for the environment. You could go to a landfill and dig around a bit to see which bags biodegrade and which don't, or you could try this experiment.

PROBLEM/PURPOSE

How do certain environmental conditions affect how disposable grocery bags biodegrade?

EXPERIMENT SUMMARY

You'll place plastic and paper bags in a variety of environments to see how quickly the bags decompose.

WHAT YOU NEED

- ▶ **4 biodegradable plastic grocery bags (from the same store)**
- ▶ **4 nonbiodegradable plastic grocery bags (from the same store)**
- ▶ **4 paper shopping bags (from the same store)**
- ▶ **9 wooden stakes**
- ▶ **Sunny location in a yard**
- ▶ **Mallet**
- ▶ **Pitch fork**
- ▶ **Use of a compost pile**
- ▶ **Shovel**
- ▶ **3 containers, 3-gallon (11.4 L) capacity**
- ▶ **Water**

EXPERIMENTAL PROCEDURE

1. Secure one of each of the bags to the same sunny location in a yard. Use two stakes to keep each of the bags from blowing away.

If you don't have a compost pile, ask neighbors or friends if they have one you can borrow. You won't have enough time to create one from scratch.

2. Dig three holes 1 foot (30.5 cm) deep with the shovel. Place one of each of the bags in each hole and fill in the holes with the dirt. Use the remaining stakes to mark the locations of the holes.

3. Use the pitch fork to help you place one of each of the bags in the middle of the compost pile. Rake the removed compost material back over the bags.

4. Fill each of the three 3-gallon (11.4 L) containers to the brim with water.

5. Place the remaining three bags in the containers.

6. Leave the bags where they are for three to four months. If you have less than two months to do this experiment, try it with different kinds of paper products instead.

7. Record the changes in each of the bags in each of the locations.

CONCLUSION

Be very descriptive when comparing the bags in each of the locations. Describe what they looked liked, whether or not there were holes in the bags or pieces missing. Which bags decomposed the best? The worst? Did one type of bag perform better than the rest in each of the locations, or were the results mixed?

WHAT ELSE YOU CAN DO

● Try this same experiment with different kinds of paper (looseleaf, newspaper, card stock, etc.).

Eggstraordinary!

Eggs get a bad rap for being quite fragile, and sure, if you bang one against something, it'll break. But what happens when you spread out the pressure that's being applied to the egg over the whole shell?

PROBLEM/PURPOSE

What is the effect of equal amounts of pressure on an eggshell's durability?

EXPERIMENT SUMMARY

You'll test the strength of an egg by applying pressure at various angles.

WHAT YOU NEED

▶ **Several eggs (raw, not boiled)**
▶ **10 volunteers**

EXPERIMENTAL PROCEDURE

1. Remove any rings from your hands. Over a sink or tray, cup an egg in one hand. Squeeze the egg as hard as you can, making sure the pressure you're applying is even all around. Record your observations. Repeat with the volunteers.

2. Interlock your fingers, and place the egg so that the top and bottom are touching inside your hands. Squeeze the egg as hard as you can from one end to another. Record your observations. Repeat this test with the volunteers.

3. Turn the egg sideways, and repeat the squeeze as in step 2. Record your observations. Repeat with the volunteers.

4. Apply force to just one side of the egg by tapping it on a hard object. Record your observations.

CONCLUSION

Which procedures cracked the egg's shell? Did you notice if certain angles were stronger than others? Show your results in a table.

TAKE A CLOSER LOOK

● Eggs are convex surfaces, which means they have a surface that curves outward. When you squeeze an egg, the pressure you're applying spreads out evenly over the egg, and the egg can withstand over 130 pounds (59 kg) of pressure when evenly applied. Ancient Romans realized that the shape of the egg was the key to its strength, and this helped them to develop rounded arches that could span a large space with little support. This then led to the development of the dome-shaped building.

WHAT ELSE YOU CAN DO

● Test the eggshells themselves. Break two eggs so that they're halved, top to bottom. Rinse the shells, and let them dry. Use scissors to trim off any jagged edges. Place the four eggshell halves flat-side down in a square shape, and carefully add weight to them, such as books, to see how much weight they're able to withstand.

Take a Closer Look:
Science Fiction Movie Bloopers

"Sure is quiet out here...."

You and your friends are staring at a dark, silent movie screen. The only light is from the twinkling of faraway stars from faraway galaxies. Suddenly a deafening roar fills the movie theater and WHOOOSH!, an intergalactic space fighter races onto the screen with lasers blasting, zip zip, zap zap! It's a spectacular sight—enough to take your breath away and lead you and your friends to imagine what space travel may be like in the future. But no matter how awesome the sight of a spacecraft in a really cool science fiction movie is, there's almost always something incredibly wrong with the sound. As we all know, there's no air in space. And unfortunately for movie directors, in order to make a sound, you need air to carry the sound waves. So, no air...no noise. Hence, no zoom, boom, blam, whoosh, blast, zip, or zap in space. Just silence. Movie directors probably know this, but must figure it's a pretty boring science fiction movie without all those awesome sound effects. This is just one example of bad science in the movies. In fact, science bloopers abound in science fiction movies, and the closer you look, the more you find.

In most cases, science bloopers are mere oversights. Take *Star Wars*, for instance. In one of the early scenes in the movie, Luke Skywalker is watching the double sunset of his home planet. If his planet has two suns, Luke and everyone and everything on the planet should have two shadows. But they don't! Someone didn't do his homework.

In other instances, science is changed for a more dramatic movie-going experience. In *Jurassic Park,* there were dinosaurs who were extremely intelligent and scheming hunters, whereas all evidence points to these dinosaurs being no smarter than house pets. And remember the Dilophosaurus who could flare its neck and spit a stream of nerve gas to blind its prey? There's no evidence it could do either. But it sure made for an interesting movie moment. And how come every time there's a natural disaster in a movie, it happens in a big city such as New York? Killer asteroids all seem to aim for the big cities in disaster movies, when it's much more likely that asteroids, if they were to fall to Earth, would fall in an ocean, since there's much more ocean than land on Earth. Or, even if an asteroid did hit land, why not land in a village populated mostly by sheep? Because it's not as much fun as watching big buildings blow up.

Speaking of asteroids, the movie *Armageddon*, which tells the story of a rag-tag bunch of men who save Earth from a giant asteroid, is rife with science bloopers. Lack of gravity is forgotten about, the science of asteroids is ignored, and the whole premise of how the heroes save the Earth from the giant asteroid is absurd. "So what," you say. "That's why they call it science FICTION!" Well, you're right. But it does help prove that even though movies make things look as if they're really happening, it doesn't always mean those things can happen. Plus, you can amaze your friends and family with your scientific knowledge, and point out the goof-ups you find. It can be fun, but save your critique for after the movie... otherwise you may get kicked out of the theater!

Not coming to a theater near you:
The Asteroid that Landed Harmlessly in the Ocean!

Powerful Produce

Which has more zing, a lemon or a tomato? Or is it a potato? Fruits and vegetables can act as conductors for electric current when included in a circuit. Raid the refrigerator for this experiment, and show your family how fun it can be to play with your food.

PROBLEM/PURPOSE

Which fruit or vegetable conducts electricity the best?

EXPERIMENT SUMMARY

You'll make a complete circuit that tests each piece of produce for its ability to generate and conduct electric current.

WHAT YOU NEED

- ▶ Assortment of same-sized fruits and vegetables (try lemons, limes, oranges, grapefruits, tomatoes, turnips, potatoes, and onions)
- ▶ 1-inch (2.5 cm) piece of copper
- ▶ 1-inch (2.5 cm) piece of zinc
- ▶ Multimeter (battery tester) or small lightbulbs with varying wattages
- ▶ 2 pieces of copper wire with the ends stripped (if using lightbulbs)
- ▶ pH paper

EXPERIMENTAL PROCEDURE

1. Insert the pieces of zinc and copper into opposite ends of your first piece of produce, leaving ¼ inch (6 mm) of the metal exposed.

The zinc and copper should not touch each other.

2. Clip the negative end of the battery tester to the exposed piece of zinc, and clip the positive end of the battery tester to the copper. Or, if using lightbulbs, attach a piece of copper wire to each piece of metal and the lightbulb. The zinc is the negative pole and the copper is the positive pole, as electrons leave the zinc and travel through the circuit to reenter the cell through the copper.

3. Record the reading on the battery tester in your journal. If using lightbulbs, record the highest watt bulb you can light when hooked to the circuit.

4. Disconnect the fruit or vegetable from the circuit. Slice it open and wet a strip of pH paper with its juice. Follow the instructions on the package of pH paper for determining the pH value, and record the pH in your notebook.

5. Repeat this procedure for each of the remaining pieces of produce.

CONCLUSION

Which fruit or vegetable produced the strongest reading for current? How did the more acidic foods (lower pH values), such as lemons and tomatoes, compare with less acidic foods (higher pH values)?

TAKE A CLOSER LOOK

● The metals copper and zinc have a loose hold on their electrons (the negatively charged particles that help make up atoms), and so they pass them back in forth when there's a conducting material between them. This movement of electrons is what's known as "electric current." The acid in lemons and tomatoes also reacts with zinc, and a transfer of electrons will take place between them. In this way, a lemon performs as a cell, which is the proper scientific term for what we commonly think of as a battery. When copper is introduced into the fruit or vegetable, a complete circuit is created, with the electrons moving from the positive pole to the negative pole. You measured this flow with the multimeter or lightbulbs.

● Technically, a "battery" is defined as a group of cells that are connected together.

WHAT ELSE YOU CAN DO

● Compare different sizes of the same fruit or vegetable to see how that affects the amount of current that's generated through the circuit.

"When I do another science fair project, I'll definitely plan ahead and not procrastinate. I encourage anyone who's doing a science fair project not to put everything off until the last minute because you might get so interested in the topic that you'll wish you had more time!"
—Julie Claire Guest, 6th grader

"Set time goals and stick to them. The most important thing, though, is to pick a project that interests you."
—Penn Tarleton, 6th grader

Pointing North

In the time before our roads became littered with signs telling us which exit to get off, a compass could be the difference between life and death. Even today, a compass can be a truly helpful device when you're out hiking or exploring. This simple experiment helps teach you how a compass works.

PROBLEM/PURPOSE

How does a compass work?

EXPERIMENT SUMMARY

Using easy-to-find items, you'll be able to create a compass that'll help you understand how it works.

WHAT YOU NEED

- ▶ **Sewing needle or straight pin, approximately 1 inch (2.5 cm) long**
- ▶ **Bar or refrigerator magnet**
- ▶ **Small cup**
- ▶ **Water**
- ▶ **Small circular piece of cork (from a wine cork)**
- ▶ **Compass**

EXPERIMENTAL PROCEDURE

1. Hold the needle in one hand and the magnet in the other. Move the magnet across the needle, rubbing in the same direction 10 to 20 times. Make sure that when you run the magnet down the length of the pin, you're using the same part of the magnet and that you're lifting the magnet after one stroke, and then returning it to where you started before rubbing again. In other words, you're not rubbing the magnet back and forth.

2. Fill the cup with water, and place the cork in the cup. You're testing how the cork sits in the water.

3. Get an adult assistant to help you. Force the needle all the way through the cork so it sticks out both sides.

4. Place the cork in the water. The needle needs to be parallel to the surface and resting on the surface of the water.

5. Observe what happens when the water settles.

6. Test the accuracy of your compass by comparing its reading to the reading of the real compass.

CONCLUSION

When you rubbed the magnet down the length of the needle, iron molecules in the pin became magnetized. How did your compass compare to the manufactured one?

● A compass needle points toward the magnetic North Pole, which lies in northern Canada (not to be confused with the geographical North Pole). And if you really want to get technical, the north pole of the compass is actually attracted to Earth's magnetic South Pole and vice versa. Why? Because opposite poles attract.

● Your compass can be used anywhere there's a puddle of water. All you really need to make a compass is a lightweight magnet (in this case, a magnetized needle) balanced on a point that provides very little friction (the water). A compass works because Earth has a weak magnetic field that's created by its magnetic core. This core is like a large magnet surrounded by a magnetic field that extends beyond our atmosphere. However, this field is weak, which is why the magnet in the compass has to be lightweight and frictionless.

WHAT ELSE YOU CAN DO

● Research how to take bearings on a compass, and create a treasure hunt for a friend to complete with a treasure map.

● Determine what objects interfere with your compass' reading, such as paper, a watch, a pencil, or another magnet.

Take a Closer Look:
Science Math Continued

Calculating Averages

During your science fair project you'll often need to repeat your experiment several times to eliminate errors in your technique and to make sure that your measurements are valid and not just a fluke. Now, what do you do with all those numbers? Well, since your measurements won't be identical each time you perform your test, it's necessary to average the numbers. To do this, add all the numbers together and divide by the total number of values. For example, if you scored 70 out of 100 on your first science test, 90 on the second, and 74 on the third, your average test score would be 78 (70 + 90 + 74 = 234; 234 ÷ 3 = 78).

What's the Difference Between Mean, Median, and Mode?

The average of a set of numbers is also known as the mean. However, sometimes the mean doesn't give you enough information. For example, suppose a group of 10 students scored the following on a science test: 87, 80, 92, 98, 87, 95, 57, 87, 85, and 78. To calculate the mean or average, add the numbers together and divide by 10. The mean score was 84.6. Notice, however, that most of the test scores were higher than the average. The lowest score, 57, really pulled down the average. In this instance, it might be useful to present the median number as well as the mean. To find the median, arrange the numbers in order: 57, 78, 80, 85, 87, 87, 87, 92, 95, 98. Then, find the number in the middle. If there's an even number of values, such as in this example, add the two middle values together (85 + 87) and divide by 2. The median is 86. This calculation eliminates extreme values that may mess up your average. Another calculation you may find useful in reporting your measurements is the mode. This is simply the value that occurs most frequently in your set of measurements. In the above example, the mode would also be 87 because it occurs three times. The mode is often used when dealing with qualitative data, such as responses in a taste-test: sour, sweet, or salty. The mode would be the response that occurred most frequently.

Remote Control Science

Our sense of sight is pretty important, and our eyes do a pretty good job of helping us interpret a lot of what's going on around us. But what we're seeing is only a small part of what's called the *electromagnetic spectrum*. The wavelengths of electromagnetic radiation that we can see are called light, and they include the colors in a rainbow. This experiment attempts to figure out what the properties are of another kind of electromagnetic radiation that we can't see.

PROBLEM/PURPOSE

How does infrared radiation compare to visible light?

EXPERIMENT SUMMARY

You'll discover how infrared radiation behaves compared to visible light, using a television remote control and a flashlight.

WHAT YOU NEED

- ▶ **Television with a remote control**
- ▶ **Use of a dark room**
- ▶ **Tape measure**
- ▶ **Masking tape**
- ▶ **Flashlight**
- ▶ **An assistant**
- ▶ **Piece of plywood, about the size of the television**
- ▶ **Large glass of water**
- ▶ **Large glass of milk**
- ▶ **Several sheets of white paper**
- ▶ **Powder**

EXPERIMENTAL PROCEDURE

1. Read the instructions that came with your television set to make sure your remote control uses infrared radiation to send its signals. Most remote controls made from the 1980s to today use this technology.

2. Set up your testing area by making the room where your television is as dark as possible. Also, measure 8 feet (2.4 m) from the front of the television, and mark the location with a piece of tape.

3. Stand at the tape mark, and make sure your flashlight and remote control work.

4. Have your assistant stand 4 feet (1.2 m) away from you with the piece of plywood. Have the assistant stand off to the side and hold up the piece of plywood directly in front of the television.

5. Turn on the flashlight, and have your assistant tell you what she observes. Record the observation.

6. Point the remote control at the television and try to turn it on. Record what happens.

7. Have your assistant move 2 feet (.6 m) toward you. Repeat steps 5 and 6.

8. Have your assistant move 1 foot (30.5 cm) toward you. Repeat steps 5 and 6.

9. Have your assistant place the plywood directly in front of you. Repeat steps 5 and 6.

10. Stand at your tape mark, and place the large glass of water directly in front of the flashlight. Turn on the flashlight, and record what you see on the television screen (the television should be off).

11. Place the glass of water directly in front of the remote control, and try to turn on the television. Record what happens.

12. Repeat steps 10 and 11 with the glass of milk.

13. Stand at the tape mark, and place a single sheet of white paper in front of the flashlight. Aim the flashlight at the television (the television should be off) and turn the flashlight on. Record what you see on the screen and around the room.

14. Add a second piece of paper over the first, and repeat step 13. Keep adding sheets of paper until you have seven sheets of paper in front of the flashlight.

15. Repeat steps 13 and 14 with the remote control. Record what happens.

16. For the final test, make sure you have your parents' permission to do this before continuing. Have your assistant blow powder in the room between you and the television. Make sure it's nice and cloudy in there.

17. Point the flashlight at the darkened television screen, and record what you see.

18. Repeat with the remote control, and record what happens.

CONCLUSION

What interfered with the flashlight? What stopped the infrared beam from turning on the television? Create a chart that compares how each of the two forms of electromagnetic radiations performed in each of the tests. Once you have your data, discuss the differences and what may account for them. Your research will also help you with writing about how the two forms of radiation are different.

TAKE A CLOSER LOOK

● A wavelength is the distance between one wave crest and the next. The electromagnetic spectrum includes radio waves, microwaves, infrared, visual light, ultraviolet, X-rays, and gamma rays, with radio waves having the longest wavelengths, and gamma rays having the shortest.

● "Infrared" means "below the red" because it appears right at the

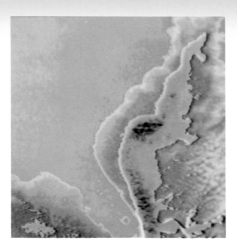

An infrared photograph of the Gulf Stream

end of the visible spectrum (just below red). Infrared radiation is thermal radiation, which means that even though we can't see it, we certainly feel it as heat! So, it's really our sense of touch that helps us sense infrared radiation. But since the type of infrared radiation used in remote controls is so close to the visual spectrum, it's really not hot at all.

● There are special scanners and camera film that can detect infrared radiation, and they have a broad number of uses, including:

▶ Determining the temperature of objects

▶ Locating heat leaks in buildings

▶ Finding hidden tumors in the body

▶ Finding diseased vegetation in a forest

▶ Detecting stars we can't see

▶ Recording environmental changes on Earth

▶ Getting pictures of objects covered by a haze

▶ Helping sharp-shooters see their targets

Brrrrrr, Bring Back the Clouds!

Have you ever noticed that it seems like the coldest nights of the season are also the clearest? Does a layer of clouds in the sky make a difference on nightly temperatures?

PROBLEM/PURPOSE

What effect does cloud cover have on nighttime temperatures?

EXPERIMENT SUMMARY

Observe the night sky for 14 nights in a row (or longer), and determine if there's a relationship between cloud cover and temperature.

WHAT YOU NEED

▶ **Notebook**
▶ **Pen**
▶ **Thermometer**

EXPERIMENTAL PROCEDURE

1. Find a location outside your home that will shelter the thermometer from any wind.

2. On night 1, check the thermometer at sunset, and record the time and temperature in your notebook.

3. Look up at the sky and estimate the percentage of cloud cover you see. A solid sky of clouds would equal 100 percent; a sky with equal amounts of clouds and open spaces would be 50 percent; a few wispy clouds in an otherwise clear sky might be 10 percent. Use your best judgement, and write visual descriptions along with the percentages so you'll be able to stay consistent with your estimates over the 14 days.

4. Go outside again before you go to sleep, and record the temperature and percentage of cloud coverage. Note the time.

5. Repeat steps 2 through 4 for the next 13 nights. You should make your observations at the same times you recorded on the first night.

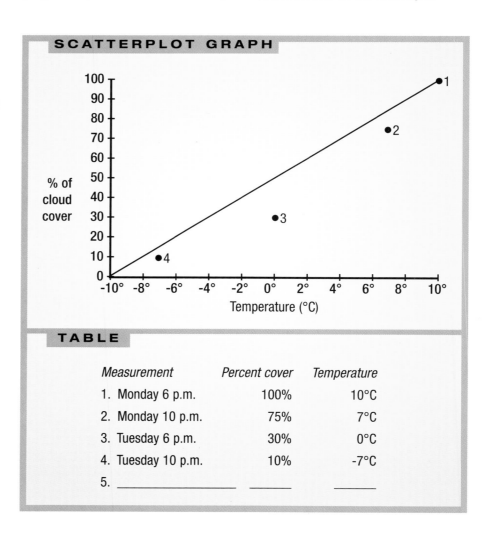

SCATTERPLOT GRAPH

% of cloud cover vs. Temperature (°C)

TABLE

Measurement	Percent cover	Temperature
1. Monday 6 p.m.	100%	10°C
2. Monday 10 p.m.	75%	7°C
3. Tuesday 6 p.m.	30%	0°C
4. Tuesday 10 p.m.	10%	-7°C
5. _____	_____	_____

CONCLUSION

According to your data, did clouds act like a blanket, keeping the temperatures warmer? If you didn't have many nights with a lot of cloud cover, extend your experiment for another week. Record your data in a scatterplot graph like the example on page 72. Once you complete the scatterplot graph, extend a line diagonally from the lower left-hand corner of the graph to the upper right-hand corner. If your points fall close to the line in most cases then there is a correlation between cloud cover and temperature. The longer you extend the experiment, the greater your chances of getting a valid result.

TAKE A CLOSER LOOK

● Clouds are simply masses of water vapor that have condensed around particles in the atmosphere as a result of warm air cooling and becoming more dense. At night, the earth continues to radiate heat that rises from its surface into the atmosphere in parcels called *thermals*. When there are no clouds, this warm air dissipates. But when clouds are present, it's like a blanket has been tossed into the sky—the water vapor in the clouds absorbs the rising heat and traps it. Heat is then radiated from the clouds back down to the earth, keeping temperatures mild at night. The amount that clouds affect temperatures on earth depends on the cloud's type and location in the

CLOUD CHART

Cirrus

Cumulus

Stratus

Cumulonimbus

Stratocumulus

Nimbostratus

atmosphere. Thick, low-lying clouds will hold more heat near the earth's surface, whereas thin, high clouds will have little influence on surface temperatures.

● What defines a "clear sky"?

Meteorologists use the following percentages for categorizing cloud cover:

▶ Overcast = greater than 90 percent of the sky is covered with clouds

▶ Broken = 50 to 90 percent of the sky is covered with clouds

▶ Scattered = 10 to 50 percent of the sky is covered with clouds

▶ Clear = less than 10 percent of the sky has clouds

WHAT ELSE YOU CAN DO

● Go one step further and keep track of the cloud types that you see in the night sky, and see if you can predict the next day's weather. You'll need a cloud chart (see above), and you'll need to observe the direction they come from.

The Power of Electromagnets

An electromagnet uses electricity to create a magnetic field by running an electric current through a wire. Electromagnets are used in VCRs, tape players, television cameras, computer disk drives, many motors, and even doorbells. In junkyards, super-strong electromagnets are hooked onto cranes to move cars and large pieces of scrap metal. This experiment first shows you how to create an electromagnet (not one strong enough to lift your family's car), then you'll attempt to find out what makes one stronger.

PROBLEM/PURPOSE

What factors make an electromagnet stronger?

WHAT YOU NEED

- Needle-nose pliers
- 18-gauge wire
- 6 alligator clips
- 2 non-alkaline batteries, 6-volt
- 1 iron bolt
- Use of a wooden table
- 2 boxes of paper clips
- Aluminum foil molded to the shape and size of the iron bolt
- Piece of wood whittled to the shape and size of the iron bolt
- Piece of plastic cut to the shape and size of the iron bolt

EXPERIMENT SUMMARY

You'll test the strength of an electromagnet three ways. First you'll see how the number of batteries used affects strength. Then you'll test how the number of times you wrap the coil around the core affects strength. Finally, you'll test the core itself to see how it affects strength.

Warning: If the wire gets hot to the touch at any point, disconnect the wire from the battery right away and let it cool off!

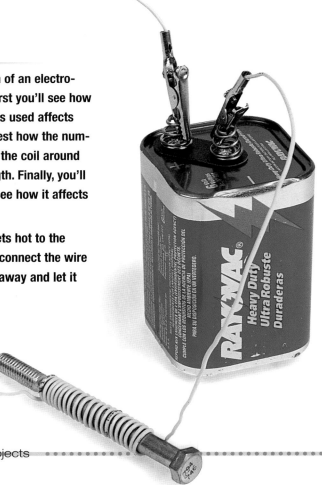

EXPERIMENTAL PROCEDURE

1. Cut three pieces of wire with the needle-nose pliers to the following lengths: 8 inches (20.3 cm), 2 feet (61 cm), and 5 feet (1.5 m).

2. Have an adult expose the ends of the three wires and attach the alligator clips.

3. Wrap the 2-foot (61 cm) wire around the iron bolt 10 times, leaving extra wire to hook to the battery. Hook one alligator clip to the negative side of one of the batteries and the other clip to the positive end.

4. Place the bolt 1 inch (2.5 cm) away from a pile of paper clips, and record how many paper clips the bolt attracts. Repeat two more times, and average the three results. Make sure you're doing this on a wooden table.

5. Have an adult connect two batteries by hooking the 8-inch (20.3 cm) wire to the positive of battery #1 and the negative side of battery #2. Then take the iron core with the 2-foot (61 cm) wire still coiled around it, and attach one end to the negative of battery #1, and the other end to the positive of battery #2.

6. Place the bolt 1 inch (2.5 cm) away from the pile of paper clips, and record how many paper clips the bolt attracts. Repeat two more times, and average the three results.

7. Remove the second battery from the electromagnet. Remove the 2-foot (61 cm) wire from the core.

8. To test how the number of times a wire is coiled around the core affects strength, use the 5-foot (1.5 m) wire. Wrap it around the core 20 times, and attach it to one of the batteries. Place the bolt 1 inch (2.5 cm) away from the pile of paper clips, and record how many paper clips the bolt attracts. Repeat two more times, and average the three results.

9. Remove the wire from the battery, and wrap the wire around the bolt 10 more times (30 total). Hook up the wires to the battery, and test how many paper clips the core attracts. Record your results, and repeat two more times and figure out the average.

10. Repeat step 9 so you have a total of 40 coils. Record your results.

11. For the final test, you'll use the iron bolt again. Coil the 2-foot (61 cm) wire around the bolt 10 times, and test how many paper clips it attracts. Record your results, and repeat two more times to obtain an average.

12. Repeat step 11 for the wood piece, plastic piece, and aluminum foil. Record your results.

CONCLUSION

Record the results of the three experiments to come up with what would be the strongest electromagnet. Would more batteries be better than less? How many coils would you suggest using? What material should the core be made out of?

TAKE A CLOSER LOOK

● An electromagnet forms when electric current flows through a wire and produces a magnetic field around the wire. This link between electricity and magnetism was first noticed in 1820 by Hans Christian Oersted, when he observed that an electric current in a wire deflected the needle of a compass.

● The magnetic-field strength produced by an electromagnet depends on the number of coils, the size of the current, and how magnetic the

core is. The more power supplied to the electromagnet, the stronger it will be. The number of coils also determines the strength of the field. The magnetic field around a single wire is quite weak, so coiling the wire around an iron core increases the strength of the electromagnet by concentrating the magnetic field. Though wood, plastic, and aluminum aren't magnetic, there would still be some magnetic field, but not much. Were you able to pick up any paper clips with the wood, plastic, or aluminum cores?

WHAT ELSE YOU CAN DO

● Research how electromagnets are used in everyday life, from doorbells to motors, and create your own uses for an electromagnet.

The Great Fabric Test

Most expedition teams planning to climb the world's highest mountains pack a careful selection of clothing mostly made from synthetic, or man-made, fibers. They choose these new fabrics because they're lightweight, durable, and warm. But how do these fabrics (mixes of polyester, lycra, fleece, and nylon) compare with the world's ancient standbys, wool and cotton, when it comes to getting wet? Try this experiment to find out which fabrics dry the fastest and hold the least moisture—an important concern on rainy day hikes, mountain treks, or anytime you're outdoors for a long period of time.

PROBLEM/PURPOSE

Which fabrics retain moisture the longest?

EXPERIMENT SUMMARY

You'll saturate a collection of synthetic and natural fabric samples, and compare the drying times of each.

WHAT YOU NEED

- Same-sized squares of the following fabrics: polyester, nylon, fleece, cotton, wool, denim, and any blends of these.
- Water
- Bucket/dishpan
- Clothesline and clothespins
- Permanent marker
- Water-based marker
- Sheet of paper

EXPERIMENTAL PROCEDURE

1. Fill the dishpan or bucket with water and take all of your materials outside to the clothesline. If you have a clothesline indoors, then you can fill a nearby sink or bathtub with water instead.

2. Use the permanent marker to label each piece of fabric according to what it's made of. If you have some blends of fibers, then label them with the percentage of each component material (e.g., 30-percent cotton, 70-percent polyester).

3. Submerge the fabric samples in the bucket of water and let them soak for 20 minutes. Stir them around a few times while they're soaking to be sure each piece gets thoroughly wet.

4. Set up a chart in your notebook with a column for the fabric type and a column for drying times.

5. Note the time in your notebook, and hang all of the samples on the clothesline so that they're not touching.

6. After 15 minutes, feel each of the samples to see if any are dry yet. If you find a dry sample, record the time on the chart in your notebook. Check the samples for dryness every 15 minutes after the initial survey. If it's a hot, sunny day, or if there's a strong breeze, you may need to start checking the fabric samples sooner and continue checking them more frequently. As the fabric samples become nearly dry, you'll need to check them as often as every five minutes.

7. After the fabrics are dry, redo the experiment at least two more times on different days.

Note: Here's a suggestion for checking the dryness of a fabric sample: color a circle with the water-based marker on the sheet of paper. Press the bottom edge of the fabric against the circle. If the ink bleeds, there's still water in the fabric.

CONCLUSION

Compare the drying times you recorded, and put them in order from longest to shortest. Which fabric took the longest and which took the shortest amount of time to dry? What were they made of? What do the fastest drying fabrics have in common?

TAKE A CLOSER LOOK

● Clothing is an important factor for keeping comfortable when spending long periods of time outdoors. The fibers in cotton clothes will hold moisture longer than those in polypropylene or fleece. For this reason, some people prefer cotton for desert day hikes because the slowly evaporating moisture will keep you cool under the sun. Wool fibers, as in your socks, hold in heat, but will also hold a lot of water when wet, making it a good choice for dry, cold weather and a bad choice for warm, wet days. Considering that wool, cotton, and fur were the fabrics of choice for many of the world's famous explorers prior to the mid-1900s, what do you imagine they'd think of the wide range of high-tech, specialized clothing? Perhaps, a few of those fatal expedition attempts would have turned out better, and the names on today's maps would have looked a little different if these old-time explorers had some of today's technologically advanced clothing!

WHAT ELSE YOU CAN DO

● Compare how much water different fabrics absorb. Pour a measured amount of water on same-size pieces of fabric, and then measure the amount of water you can wring out of each piece.

DISPLAY TIPS

● Contact manufacturers of the different materials used in the experiment, and ask for brochures you can use on your display.

The Chilling Facts

When meteorologists talk about wind chill factor, they're not talking about the actual temperature, but rather, how cold it feels due to the wind. In other words, if it was 35°F (2°C) outside with a wind chill factor of 6°F (-14°C), it would still be 35°F (2°C) (water wouldn't freeze), but it would feel as if it were much colder. How exactly does the wind chill factor affect us?

PROBLEM/PURPOSE

What is the effect of wind chill on different inanimate objects?

EXPERIMENT SUMMARY

You'll test how quickly the same-sized containers made of different materials return to room temperature using a fan.

WHAT YOU NEED

▶ **Fan**
▶ **Cardboard strip**
▶ **8 ounce (240 mL) glass**
▶ **8 ounce (240 mL) ceramic mug**
▶ **8 ounce (240 mL) plastic cup**
▶ **8 ounce (240 mL) metal insulated mug**
▶ **Marker**
▶ **Use of a stove**
▶ **Pot**
▶ **Water**
▶ **5 thermometers**
▶ **Wristwatch**

EXPERIMENTAL PROCEDURE

1. Find a suitable place to do the experiment, preferably a room without a lot of open windows. Place the fan on the floor and then place the cardboard strip horizontally facing the fan, 18 inches (45.7 cm) away.

2. Place each container on top of the cardboard strip. The containers should be placed so that they receive the full effects of the fan.

3. Turn the fan on and test each location. Once you're sure each container is in a good position, trace each container's location with the marker onto the cardboard.

4. Boil enough water to fill the four containers with 6 ounces (180 mL).

5. Record the room temperature with one of the thermometers.

6. Once the water has boiled, carefully fill each of the containers.

7. Place the remaining thermometers in each of the containers. Record the temperatures (they should be the same).

8. Turn the fan on to its highest setting.

9. Use the watch to record how long it takes the water in each container to return to room temperature. Record the results.

10. For the second trial, repeat steps 4 through 7, but keep the fan off. Record the results.

CONCLUSION

Did the water temperature in any of the containers drop below room temperature? Which container lost its heat the quickest? Which container retained its heat the longest?

HANDY WIND CHILL CHART

Wind speed	Temperature (Celsius)							
	0°C	-5°C	-10°C	-15°C	-20°C	-25°C	-30°C	-35°C
10 kph 6 mph	-2	-7	-12	-17	-22	-27	-32	-38
20 kph 12 mph	-7	-13	-19	-25	-31	-37	-43	-50
30 kph 18 mph	-11	-17	-24	-31	-37	-44	-50	-57
40 kph 24 mph	-13	-20	-27	-34	-41	-48	-55	-62
50 kph 30 mph	-15	-22	-29	-36	-44	-51	-58	-66
60 kph 36 mph	-16	-23	-31	-38	-45	-53	-60	-68

lets heat escape more quickly. In other words, hot air rises and the cold air fills its place; this process is called *convection*, and you're quickening the process by simply blowing on the soup.

WHAT ELSE YOU CAN DO

● Do a similar experiment with six of the same containers, and wrap them in different materials (felt, fur, denim, cotton, etc.) to see which material retains heat the best when exposed to wind.

How do you account for the differences in time it took for the different containers to return to room temperature? Set up a bar graph showing the minutes it took for each container to return to room temperature with the fan off and the fan on.

TAKE A CLOSER LOOK

● The wind chill factor is really a measure of the rate of heat loss, and not an actual temperature. It tells you how quickly heat is lost due to the wind, not how cold your nose, a car, or a container will get. No matter how hard the wind is blowing, if the temperature is above 32°F (0°C) water will not freeze. Have you ever blown on your soup to cool it down? What you're actually doing is similar to the wind chill factor: you're increasing the rate at which it will cool down by increasing the movement of the air, which in turn

Under Pressure

At this very moment, you're being pushed around. No, not by some invisible guy who doesn't like you, but by air. Air, or Earth's atmosphere, pushes on each side of your body with a force equal to 1 kilogram per square centimeter (14.7 pounds per square inch) at sea level. But before you get all defensive, it's not even something you notice, since the air inside you is pushing out at the same force, evening things up. But what happens when you change that inside air pressure that's keeping you from being squashed like a bug?

PROBLEM/PURPOSE

What is the effect of air pressure on an object not supported on all sides by equal air pressure?

EXPERIMENT SUMMARY

You'll identify air pressure and how it can affect objects when you remove air pressure from inside of a can.

WHAT YOU NEED

▶ **Metal can with a cap or lid**
▶ **2 cups (.48 L) water**
▶ **Small butane burner or use of a stove**
▶ **Tongs or oven mitt**

EXPERIMENTAL PROCEDURE

1. Pour the water into the can.

2. Turn the burner on low/medium, and place the can on top of it (without the cap).

3. When the water begins to boil, keep the can on the burner for 30 seconds. Then, remove it with the tongs or the oven mitt, and turn off the burner.

4. Put the cap on the can, and let the can cool for 5 minutes.

5. Observe what happens, and record your observations in your notebook.

CONCLUSION

The empty can had equal amounts of atmospheric pressure on the outside and inside of the can. By removing the can from the heat and putting the cap on, the steam condensed back to water. This reduced the pressure inside the can, much

like a sudden drop in altitude reduces air pressure on an airplane (see Take a Closer Look). The pressure of the air on the outside of the can became greater than the pressure inside.

TAKE A CLOSER LOOK

● Air pressure is the force exerted on you by the weight of tiny air molecules. And, even though they're invisible, they still have weight and take up space. This weight doesn't crush you because you have air inside your body that balances out the pressure outside. As you change your altitude, air pressure also changes, and the further up you go, the more air pressure decreases. Take a ride in an elevator and go to the top floor without stopping along the way (the longer the ride, the better). What happens to your ears? They pop. Why? Because when you change altitude, the air pressure also changes. So when you ride up in an elevator or take off on an airplane, your body's moving quickly from a place of high pressure to a place of less pressure, and the air in your ears expands until it escapes. POP!

DISPLAY TIPS

● Perform this experiment on different kinds of cans, and bring the results to the fair.

Take a Closer Look:
What Scientists Study

If there's a phenomenon out there, chances are there's a scientist studying it. And most likely there'll be a name for studying that phenomenon, even if it's something as strange as bell ringing! In fact, the study of bell ringing is called *campanology*. "Ology" is a suffix that comes from the Greek word "logos" (which means "word" or "speech"), and scientists have been slapping it onto the ends of words to name their sciences for over 400 years. So, we end up with words like "biology" (the study of life and living organisms) and "meteorology" (the study of weather). But now, ladies and gentlemen, a list of some rather unusual sciences along with their unusual names.

Science	The Study of...	Science	The Study of...
Aerolithology	Meteors	Nidology	Birds' nests
Agrostology	Grass	Olfactology	Odors (see page 28)
Anemology	Wind		
Cryology	Snow and ice	Ombrology	Rain (Say this one out loud... sound familiar?)
Graphology	Handwriting		
Helminthology	Worms (especially internal worms)	Oreology	Mountains (not mountains of cookies)
Hemipterology	Bedbugs	Orthopterology	Cockroaches
Hippology	Horses (but horseology is not the study of hippos)	Punnology	Puns (Isn't that marbleous!)
		Pyrology	Fire
Ichnology	Fossil footprints	Rhinology	Noses (not just big ones)
Ichthyology	Fish		
Koniology	Atmospheric dust	Speleology	Caves
		Thaumatology	Miracles
Myrmecology	Ants	Trichology	Hair
Nephology	Clouds	Vexillogy	Flags

Up on the Rooftop

Ever notice that your summer clothes tend to be lightweight and often white or light in color, while your winter clothes are usually thicker and darker in color? Color and temperature have a connection. Look around your neighborhood at the color of the roofs. Are the majority light or dark colored? Now think about where you live and what the temperature is like most of the time. With this experiment you'll figure out how best to dress a house in your neighborhood.

PROBLEM/PURPOSE

What is the effect of the color of roofing on a house's temperature?

EXPERIMENT SUMMARY

You'll create five cardboard homes with different-colored roofs and then compare the inside temperature of the boxes throughout the day.

WHAT YOU NEED

- ▶ 5 medium-sized cardboard boxes (exactly the same size)
- ▶ Nail
- ▶ Black roofing shingles
- ▶ White roofing shingles
- ▶ Red roofing shingles
- ▶ Gray roofing shingles
- ▶ Brown roofing shingles
- ▶ Duct tape
- ▶ 5 pieces of string
- ▶ 5 outdoor thermometers

EXPERIMENTAL PROCEDURE

1. Make a nail-sized hole in the center of the top of each box.

2. Thread a piece of string through the hole in the first box, and make a knot in the string (above the hole in the box) to keep it from falling through. Tie strings like this in the remaining four boxes.

3. Tie a thermometer to each string.

4. Cover the top and sides of the first box with one layer of the black roofing shingles. Use duct tape to hold them to the box, and be sure to cover any open spaces (you may need to overlap some of the shingles).

white sidewalks offer a cooler place to stand. It's also the same principle for why white clothes are more popular in the summer and in warm climates than dark clothes. And, when it comes to roofing materials, it explains why homes in warm climates tend to have light-colored roofing shingles, while homes in colder regions use darker shingles.

5. Cover the remaining boxes in the same manner, but use a different colored set of shingles for each new box.

6. Set all five of the boxes close together in a sunny place in your yard, driveway, deck, or patio. All of the boxes must be on the same type of surface and face the same direction in the sun. Avoid placing them in the shadow of a tree or other object that may interfere with sunlight as the day progresses. If it's windy, you may need to weigh the boxes down, but be sure to use the same material for all the boxes.

7. Check the temperature inside each box once every hour, and record your data. Note any changes in the amount of sunlight that's hitting the boxes. Also, record the time with each reading and the final temperature for each box one hour after the sun has set.

CONCLUSION

Compare the temperatures of all the boxes. Are the average temperatures for any one box higher than the others? Which box recorded the lowest temperatures? Were all of the boxes consistently in the sun or did they become shaded? Were there any other factors that may have affected your results (i.e., the wind picked up and blew over two of the boxes)? Which house cooled down the quickest as the sun set? Which one cooled down the slowest? Which roofing would you suggest for cold regions? Warm regions?

TAKE A CLOSER LOOK

● Have you ever noticed how hot a black road gets on a sunny day versus the white sidewalk? Part of this is a matter of color. Black is the result of all of the visible light wavelengths from the sun being absorbed into a surface, while white is the result of all of the visible light wavelengths being reflected away from a surface. Colors in between are the result of certain visible light wavelengths being reflected while others are absorbed. The more light that's absorbed, the warmer an object will get—hence, black roads practically burn your feet on bright sunny days, while

WHAT ELSE YOU CAN DO

● If you can't get your hands on roofing shingles, try painting each box with a base coat of primer and then follow with a different color for each box. Or, try painting metal buckets with primer, and then apply different-colored paint to each bucket. Fill each bucket with water, and measure the temperature of the water throughout the day.

● Explore other ways that color can be an advantage. For example, black paint on south-facing walls (which stay sunny most of the day) absorbs heat and can be a way of incorporating passive solar energy in a home. Black pipes filled with water absorb sunlight in many solar homes and produce heat and hot water without electricity. And have you ever noticed the color of solar panels?

DISPLAY TIPS

● Bring one of your cardboard homes to the fair to display. Also, photograph the houses and their location to show they received the same amount of sunlight.

Hooked on Hydrophonics!

Whales do it. Dolphins do it. In fact, communicating under-water is quite effective, and it's even possible for you to get your point across underwater without using a megaphone. Hydrophonics is the study of underwater sound, and you'll study the effects water has on sound with this experiment.

PROBLEM/PURPOSE

What effect does water have on sound?

EXPERIMENT SUMMARY

You'll test the ability of sound to travel underwater, using a pen and a swimming pool. Don't do this experiment if you can't swim, and have an adult standing by.

WHAT YOU NEED

▶ Access to a high school or college swimming pool (or one that is 25 yards [22.5 m]), preferably during a quiet time
▶ An assistant to record observations
▶ Measuring tape
▶ Masking tape
▶ 5 volunteers who can swim
▶ Life jackets or floats to rest on in the deep water
▶ Pen with a lid that locks on (see photo)

EXPERIMENTAL PROCEDURE

1. Prior to the experiment, you and your assistant will stretch the measuring tape out the length of the pool and measure off 3-foot (.9 m) intervals. Mark these on the side of the pool with tape.

2. You and your first volunteer enter the pool at opposite ends, and stand or float touching the wall on the ends. The person in the deep end should rest on a life jacket or float to avoid splashing and making noise.

3. Ask the volunteer to close his eyes for the test. Remove the cap of the pen, but don't take the cap all the way off.

4. When the pool is quiet and you're ready, snap the pen top back on the pen. This will make a small clicking noise.

5. Ask the volunteer what he heard, and have your assistant record the observation, even if the volunteer heard nothing.

6. Now go underwater with your volunteer and repeat steps 4 and 5. Be sure to go underwater at the same time, wait no less than a few seconds and snap the pen top on.

7. Now, move in 3 feet (.9 m) toward each other (using the tape

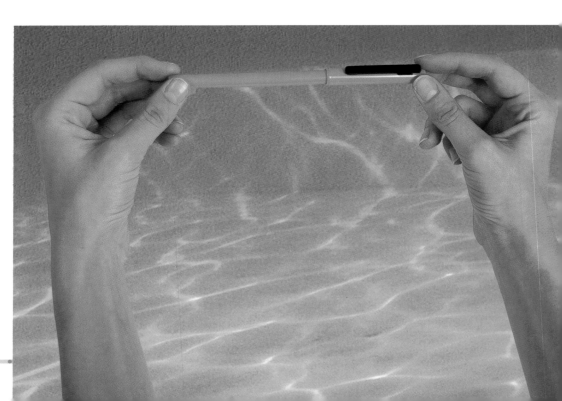

as a guide), and repeat the experiment above and below water. Your assistant will be in charge of making sure the volunteer closes his eyes and can also be the communicator between you and your volunteer while in the pool.

8. Continue moving in and repeating steps 4 through 6 until you're next to each other.

9. Repeat the entire process with other volunteers.

Note: You may not want to show the volunteers what you're using to make the snapping sound until after the experiment so that they don't know what sound to expect.

CONCLUSION

Compare the sound heard with the different distances both under and above the water surface. Was it louder above or below the water surface? At what average distance could the volunteers hear the sound underwater as opposed to above water? Show your results in a graph.

TAKE A CLOSER LOOK

● Sound waves can travel through any type of matter: solid, liquid, or gas. These waves cause particles to vibrate, and then the vibrating particles push the particles next to them and so on, and the sound waves keep on going. In fact, the closer the particles, the faster and further the sound will travel. So...since

water particles are closer together than air particles, and particles of solids are closer together than water particles, it suddenly makes sense when you think of someone putting an ear to the ground to listen for something far away.

● Sound waves travel through water at a speed of 0.9 miles per second (.5 km per second), which is $4\frac{1}{2}$ times as fast as sound traveling through air.

● Dolphins (as well as other marine mammals) can really hear what's going on around them. The part of their brain that senses and interprets what they hear is so well developed, that essentially, these marine mammals can "see" with their ears. In fact, they rely on their sense of hearing not only to com-

municate, but also to hunt and navigate in dark waters where their sense of sight isn't much help. They locate objects by making high-frequency sound waves and listening for echoes. The sound waves they make bounce off objects in the water and return in the form of an echo. This echo not only helps marine mammals determine an object's location, but also its size, shape, and speed. This process is called *echolocation.*

The Water Knows

Gravity is an invisible hand acting on the water in a stream, pulling it down to the lowest areas in the earth. Eventually, those water droplets, and the molecules and particles that manage to cling to them, will be drawn toward the ocean. But the water in a stream or river isn't moving at the same speed in different places. It's an important phenomenon canoeists, rafters, and kayakers must understand for successful river trips. "Reading the river" involves a number of observations, including anticipating where the slowest and fastest water is moving in any section of the river.

PROBLEM/PURPOSE

Where is the fastest moving current of water in a stream?

EXPERIMENT SUMMARY

Observe an improvised "boat" as it floats through four sections of a shallow stream to determine where the current is the fastest. You'll also identify the characteristics of the riverbed that support the fastest flow.

WHAT YOU NEED

- **Old pair of sneakers or boots**
- **Tape measure**
- **Saw**
- **½ x 3 x 6-inch (1.3 x 7.6 x 15.2 cm) piece of pine board or other light-weight wood**
- **Paintbrush**
- **Orange or red acrylic paint**
- **Small shallow stream**
- **Partner and an adult**
- ▶ **Sharp knife (to cut rope)**
- ▶ **Rope**
- ▶ **Notebook**
- ▶ **Meterstick**
- ▶ **Stopwatch**
- ▶ **Fishing net**

EXPERIMENTAL PROCEDURE

1. Have an adult help you cut the wood to create the boat. Paint the piece of wood a bright color so you will be able to keep track of it in the water.

2. Gather your materials and head down to the stream with your partner and adult. Don't attempt this experiment in a large river.

3. Pick out four 15-foot-long (4.5 m) sections of the stream. Section 1 should be an area that is narrow and straight; section 2 should be the widest part of the stream; section 3 should contain a curve; section 4 should have obstacles like rocks, sandbanks, or natural dams. These sections don't have to be near each other.

4. Tie a rope to a tree or other object at the beginning and end of each section (if possible, tie the rope across the stream between two trees). These will be your start and finish lines.

5. In your notebook, title a page for each section of the stream. Write under each section title a description of the physical characteristics of the stream. For example, describe the shape of the streambed, list any obstacles in the stream, note where the water appears the fastest to your eye, and record where the water looks deeper or shallower.

6. With the adult's help, measure the depth of the stream with the meterstick near each bank and in its center at the start, middle, and finish of each section. Record your measurements.

7. Begin with section 1. Stand at the start line and have your partner stand at the finish line with the stopwatch. Drop the boat in the stream and yell "go!" Your partner should start timing how long it takes the boat to cross the finish

line. As your partner is timing the boat, note the course the boat takes, and record your observations. Does it hit any obstacles or get stuck? Does it move across from one area of the stream to another on its courses. Draw a "map" of the stream section you're testing, draw the boat's path down the stream, and label it "trial 1."

8. Have your partner (or the adult you brought with you) catch the boat with the net, and repeat the test at least two more times for section 1. Average the three times you recorded, and write this number down. To calculate the speed of the boat: divide the distance (meters) by the time (seconds), and this equals the average speed of the stream in section 1.

9. Repeat steps 6 through 8 for sections 2 through 4 of the stream.

CONCLUSION

Examine the times for each section of the stream, and compare this with your observations about the shape of the stream and the course of the boat. What do the courses with the fastest times have in common? How does this relate to the observations you made about depth and stream features? What natural features seem to slow the current of a stream down? What features support a faster moving current?

TAKE A CLOSER LOOK

● Imagine you were shrunk down to the size of your boat and could sail it down the stream. Plot out the path you think would be the fastest based on what you learned from your experiment. Imagine the little drops in the stream are waterfalls and the rocks are giant boulders! What features might trap your boat and hold it in place? What channels would be the fastest? Which side would you stick to around a bend? This is the sort of thinking river guides must use to follow a fun and safe route. They must interpret how natural features will affect the flow of the water. Often, where the river widens out, the water will be calmer and slower moving than in narrower portions (depending on the slope). Where there are bends in the stream, a boater or rafter knows to stay to the outside of the bend where a deeper channel has been cut by faster moving water. The water moves more slowly along the inside edge of a bend, depositing sediment and making that side of the river more shallow—a place where boats could get hung up.

● Rivers are in a constant state of change, and every rainfall introduces new water, sediment, and debris that immediately add new elements to the water's course. No matter how experienced a boater may be on a section of river, there's always a risk involved and an element of the unknown. This is why "reading a river" is a skill boaters and rafters develop and depend on for every trip to the water—and many still toss sticks into small streams for practice.

WHAT ELSE YOU CAN DO

● Based on your observations, design a boat you think will be faster and maneuver better through a stream. Test it against your basic block of wood.

DISPLAY TIPS

● Find cool pictures of canoeists, rafters, and kayakers negotiating interesting parts of a river, such as rapids and tight turns. Use the pictures to spruce up your display.

Lighter Than Air

Have you ever wondered how many helium-filled balloons it would take to lift you into the air? This fun project may not make you airborne, but with some interesting math, you'll be able to figure out the lifting power of balloons!

PROBLEM/PURPOSE

How much weight can a helium-filled balloon lift?

EXPERIMENT SUMMARY

You'll examine the relationship between the volume of helium in a balloon and the amount of weight it can lift.

WHAT YOU NEED

▶ **10 same-sized helium-filled latex balloons**
▶ **Tape measure**
▶ **An assistant**
▶ **Nylon twine**
▶ **Scissors**
▶ **Slotted mass set [20 g (9), 10 g (1), 5 g (2)]***

* Ask your science teacher if you can borrow one, or buy one from a science supply catalog. You may also use a weight set that's not slotted, as long as you can attach twine to it.

EXPERIMENTAL PROCEDURE

1. Find the balloon with the smallest circumference with the tape measure.

2. With the help of your assistant, bleed out the helium in the rest of the balloons until they all have the same circumference as the first one.

3. Measure and cut 2 feet (60 cm) of twine. Cut a total of 10 pieces—one for each balloon.

4. Attach one twine piece to each balloon by tying it to the bottom of the balloon.

5. Attach one balloon to the 5 g weight by tying the end of the twine to it. Record your observations.

6. If the weight isn't lifted up off the table, attach another balloon to the weight and record your observations. Continue attaching balloons until the weight is lifted.

7. Once the weight is lifted, attach another 5 g weight to your group of balloons. Continue adding balloons until the total 10 g is lifted.

8. Repeat this process until all 10 balloons are attached, and you have recorded the maximum amount of weight they're able to lift. Note: All weights may not be used.

CONCLUSION

What was the maximum amount of weight lifted by the ten balloons? How many balloons did it take to lift 5 g? Follow these steps to calculate the amount of helium in your balloons:

feet, you can convert it to cubic meters by multiplying by .03.

5. One cubic foot (.03 m^3) of helium will lift about 28.2 g.

How did your results compare to the statement above? Using your results, draw a line graph showing cubic feet (or meters) of helium versus the grams of weight lifted.

TAKE A CLOSER LOOK

● Helium atoms are lighter than nitrogen and oxygen because they have fewer electrons, protons, and neutrons (the stuff that make up atoms).

● Helium weighs approximately 0.1785 grams per liter. Nitrogen, which makes up 80 percent of air, weighs 1.2506 grams per liter. A difference of approximately 1 gram may not seem like much, but as long as the helium in a balloon is lighter than the air that surrounds it, it'll float.

● Hot air balloons work in a similar way. The heat causes the air inside the balloon to expand and be pushed out the bottom of the balloon. This makes the air inside the balloon lighter than the air outside. The lifting power of the balloon is controlled by the amount of heat. In fact, if the air inside the balloon is

100 degrees hotter than the outside, the balloon will be about 25 percent lighter than the outside.

● Hydrogen is also lighter than air, weighing 0.08988 grams per liter. However, unlike helium, it's very flammable, and the slightest spark can cause an explosion.

● You've probably inhaled the helium from a balloon to produce that cool, cartoon-like voice, but have you ever wondered how that works? Since helium is lighter than the air you usually breathe, and sound is produced by vibration, helium changes the frequency of your vocal tract, causing a faster vibration and a higher-pitched sound. Whatever you do, don't inhale helium from a pressurized tank. It could cause serious medical problems!

DISPLAY TIPS

● Using your results, calculate how many balloons of the same size as yours it would take to lift a typical cat. Calculate the amount of balloons needed to lift other items—a tennis shoe, an apple, you! Display these fun facts on your display board.

1. Circumference = Pi x Diameter (Pi = 3.1415927 or 3.14). So put the circumference you used for the experiment into the equation, then divide the circumference by Pi.

2. Once you've figured out your diameter, divide by 2 to get your radius (r).

3. The volume of a sphere is 4/3(Pi)(r3). So, cube the radius you found for your balloon. Then, multiply by 3.14 and then by 4/3.

4. This is the volume of helium in one of your balloons measured in cubic feet. Once you have cubic

Following the Rain

When it rains, puddles form in potholes, and dry streambeds fill with new water. Have you ever wondered where all that rainwater goes once it lands on the earth? What happens if it lands on pavement or on a tilled acre of soil or in your backyard? Observe how different soils, plants, and ground surfaces process water.

PROBLEM/PURPOSE

How do different ground surfaces interact with rainwater?

EXPERIMENT SUMMARY

You'll fill three or more troughs with different types of ground cover, for example, pavement, grass, and exposed soil. Then you'll pour colored water on each to see how the surfaces absorb, deflect, or otherwise handle the water and the dye.

WHAT YOU NEED

- Drill, with 1-inch-diameter (2.5 cm) bit, or a saw
- 3 or more solid troughs or long window boxes (plastic or wood)
- 3 pieces of 1-inch-diameter (2.5 cm) pipe, 2 inches (5.1 cm) long
- Silicone caulk or other water-tight adhesive
- 3 or more of the following to fill the troughs halfway to the top: sand, sod, cement, straw, gravel, clay, moss
- Use of steps, or a picnic table and cement blocks
- 3 clear, wide-mouthed 1-gallon (3.8 L) jars or buckets
- Ruler
- Permanent marker
- Water
- Food coloring

EXPERIMENTAL PROCEDURE

1. Ask an adult to help you cut or drill a 1-inch (2.5 cm) hole through the center of one end of each trough.

2. Insert a section of pipe into each hole so that 1 inch (2.5 cm) or more extends from the outside of the trough. Seal each pipe in place with the caulk or other water-tight adhesive, and let set.

3. Fill each trough with the same amount of the different chosen materials (soil, sod, gravel, etc.) until level with the bottom of the pipe. Follow the package directions for mixing the cement in the trough, and let it harden.

4. Use a set of steps or a picnic table and cement blocks to elevate the solid ends of the troughs 8 inches (20.3 cm) above the pipe end of the trough. The troughs should slope downward at the same angle.

5. Draw a straight line from the bottom to the top of each jar, marking every ½ inch (1.3 cm). Place a jar on a lower step or picnic bench under each trough's pipe.

6. Slowly, pour 1 gallon (3.8 L) of colored water (add 5 drops of food coloring to each gallon [3.8 L] of water) into the same spot at the top of each trough.

7. Observe the amount and clarity of the water that collects in the jars at the bottom of the troughs.

CONCLUSION

What path did the water take as it traveled through the medium in each trough? Which collecting jar had the most water, and which had the least? What color was the water after it passed through each trough? Which jars contained dirt in the water? Which jar filled the fastest and which took the longest to fill? If you suddenly had no water in your house, which jar of water would you rather drink? Look for examples of surfaces in your neighborhood that interact with rainwater in the same manner as the mediums in the troughs you tested.

Erosion in action

TAKE A CLOSER LOOK

● As water travels over land, gravity pulls on it, encouraging it to find the easiest route to a lower point on the earth's surface. It's the same natural phenomenon that causes a dropped marble to follow the slope of a floor to the lowest point in a room. Depending on the surface it encounters, the water will percolate, or drip, down through the earth and become groundwater, or it'll rush along the earth's surface, ending up in a stream or other body of water. Clay-rich soils and plants filter water as it passes through, which explains why springs or wells, which tap into the groundwater, usually provide clear, clean drinkable water. But water that rushes down roads and over exposed farmlands picks up oil, dirt, and other chemicals, and carries them to the sewer drain or nearby stream. Eventually, most of this "runoff," and the pollutants that are suspended in it, will end up in a river, lake, or the ocean.

● The Mississippi River in the United States is a major conduit for much of the water that lands on the earth in North America. Thousands of tiny streams join up with larger ones to create a system of rivers that merge to provide the Mississippi with the 400 billion gallons (1,520 billion L) of water (and associated pollutants) that it dumps into the ocean each day. According to marine biologists, life is scarce in the "dead zone" where the Mississippi empties her toxic load into the Gulf of Mexico. Wetlands of grasses and thick soil, restored near the mouth of the river and along its major tributaries would help to filter some of the pollutants that wash down it, but the best solutions look to removing pollution from its original sources: factory discharge pipes, roads, and farmland. Unfortunately, the Mississippi is not the only river that's overloaded with pollution.

Air Matters

Imagine walking along a dirt road on a windy day when a truck passes by trailing a cloud of whirling sand, rocks, and dust. The cloud spreads out over the road and slowly dissipates, the dust and other particles settling out wherever the wind took them. Or what if you were to sit near a blooming cherry tree? You would probably find yourself covered with a coat of pollen. Dirt, pollen, seeds, pollution particles, and anything else light enough to float on the wind can be collected from the air around us and analyzed. But the type and quantity of particles you collect from the air may vary from place to place. Try this experiment to find out where the clearest and dirtiest air is in your neighborhood.

PROBLEM/PURPOSE

Where will the greatest concentration of air particles be found?

EXPERIMENT SUMMARY

Compare five days' worth of samples from test locations spread out around your neighborhood to see where the greatest amount of particles can be collected from the air.

WHAT YOU NEED

- ▶ **5 rain-free days**
- ▶ **30 large, white index cards**
- ▶ **Petroleum jelly**
- ▶ **String**
- ▶ **Nail**
- ▶ **Scissors**
- ▶ **Plastic wrap**
- ▶ **Magnifying glass**

EXPERIMENTAL PROCEDURE

1. Choose six locations in your neighborhood that have different degrees of development and potential to contribute particles (i.e., dirt, dust) to the air. For the first three sites, select locations where you expect to accumulate a lot of particles (examples include a heavily used paved road, a parking lot, a gravel/dirt road, a construction site). The last three sites should be places you expect to have the least amount of particles in the air, such as a park, a wooded area, a field, or a backyard.

2. Create six piles of five cards each. Label the cards in each pile with the location where you're going to hang them. If your card has lines on one side, label them on this side. Number the cards in each of the piles from 1 to 5.

3. Carefully punch a hole near one corner of each index card with the nail.

4. Take your cards, notebook and pen, petroleum jelly, string, and scissors to your first location during the morning on the first day.

5. Find a tree branch or other object that is 4 to 6 feet (1.2 to 1.8 m) above the ground.

6. Hang index card 1 for the first location from the object you've found. Measure the exact distance from the ground to the top of the index card once you have hung it.

7. Smear a thin layer of petroleum jelly across the blank side of the card.

8. Visit the remaining locations and hang the remaining number 1 index cards. Make sure the rest of the cards are hung at the same height as the first one you set up, and don't forget to smear the petroleum jelly across the blank sides of these cards as well.

9. At the end of the day, collect the cards from the six sites to ensure that they don't get ruined by dew or a surprise rainstorm overnight.

10. Carefully cover the petroleum jelly side of the cards with a layer of plastic wrap to protect them until the end of the experiment. Try to keep the plastic wrap smooth (i.e., wrinkle free) as you wrap it around each card.

11. Record the weather in your notebook, especially noting the amount of wind.

12. Follow steps 6 through 11 for the rest of the days of the experiment.

13. After the fifth day, it's time to analyze and compare your cards. Look over the cards, and get a general idea of the kinds of particles and matter you collected (dirt, dust, seeds, pollen, etc.). Then, sort the cards from the dirtiest to the cleanest.

14. With help from your magnifying glass, try and figure out just what kinds of particles and matter you collected in each location. Make an educated guess about what activities may have contributed the particles you collected in each location. Record your observations in a chart in your journal.

CONCLUSION

What kinds of particles did you collect in each location? According to your samples, which location proved to have the most matter swirling in the air? How did land use relate to the amount and type of particles you collected on the cards? Where would you recommend taking a nap outside in your neighborhood based on air quality?

TAKE A CLOSER LOOK

● What is dust (airborne particles)? Well, it's just about everything. Think about the dust inside your home. It might be pollen, flakes of skin (our bodies shed nearly half a million flakes of skin per minute), hair, mold, paint particles, carpet fibers, clothes lint, pet dander, bug pieces, dust mites, etc. Outside particles include car emissions, hydrocarbon waste from gas heaters, litter scraps, smokestack particles, tire rubber, soil, pollen, and much, much more! Dust has always been around, but the kind of dust that's been in our air since the Industrial Revolution can be a hazard for anything that needs to breathe.

● Here's a strange fact. According to the Environmental Protection Agency, indoor air is up to 70 times more polluted than outdoor air.

WHAT ELSE YOU CAN DO

● Collect samples to compare the effect wind has on the particle load in the air. Set samples out and compare the windy days with the calm days.

● If you have allergies, you might want to collect samples during allergy season and see how they correspond with the allergy index for each day.

● Collect samples during the winter months to see if there's a correlation between the quantity of wood smoke and ash in the air and the daily temperatures.

● Collect samples right after a rainstorm and compare them to the days preceding the rain to see the effect a good rain has on the clarity of the air.

Meteorologists Take Shelter!

How many times have you been disappointed by the local meteorologist's forecast that didn't come to pass? How about that sunny weekend that turned rainy, or the GIANT SNOWSTORM that produced only a dusting of snow that melted by mid-morning? Here's your chance to see who does better when it comes to predicting the weather.

PROBLEM/PURPOSE

How accurately can you predict the weather when compared with the local meteorologist's forecast?

EXPERIMENTAL SUMMARY

You'll make a number of basic weather instruments to aid you in observing and predicting the weather. Then you'll compare your predictions with those of a local meteorologist.

WHAT YOU NEED

▶ **Barometer (measures air pressure) (see page 96)**
▶ **Anemometer (measures wind speed) (see page 104)**
▶ **Wind vane (measures wind direction) (see page 97)**
▶ **Outdoor thermometer**
▶ **Cloud chart (see page 73)**

EXPERIMENTAL PROCEDURE

1. Once you have made and/or gathered all of your weather instruments, put them in appropriate locations for observing the weather. The

wind vane and anemometer should be placed far from buildings and other objects, in an open area. The thermometer should be set up outside, but sheltered from direct sunlight and wind. You can tape it to the inside of a white box (the white will reflect sunlight) and set it on a porch for an accurate reading. The barometer should be set up indoors in a calm area of the house where it won't get knocked over.

2. Set up the pages in your notebook to record each of the following, three times a day: date, time of day, temperature, air pressure, wind direction, wind speed, and cloud type as you have observed them. Plan to observe the weather for at least 14 days. Also include a section for the local meteorologist's daily observations, and her/his prediction for the next day's weather.

3. At the end of each day, write your weather prediction for the next day based on your observations. It'll probably take you a few days to get familiar with using your weather instruments, but after two weeks you should have a keen sense of the weather.

CONCLUSION

Look for patterns in your weather data. What changes seem to go together? Did you notice that wind from a certain direction usually brings rain? What did the cloud formations tell you about incoming weather? Were your weather observations the same or different from the local meteorologist's? Whose predictions were more accurate for the weather in your neighborhood? If your observations were different from the meteorologist's, what land features and other factors do you suspect influenced the differences? Are there changes you would make to the designs of the weather instruments to make them more accurate or easier to use? If you were to do the experiment again, are there other weather variables you would measure to make your predictions more accurate? Compare the average of correct weather predictions between you and the meteorologist.

TAKE A CLOSER LOOK

● Wind direction, air pressure, temperature, and cloud cover are basic factors that interact to produce the weather in your region at any given time of day. Careful observation of these factors can forewarn the type of weather that's headed your way. Wind from warmer, wetter regions will bring moisture to your area and may produce precipitation if it meets up with a significantly colder mass of air. Wind from arctic regions will often move in quickly as the colder, denser air mass pushes out the lighter, warmer air mass. Where cold and warm air masses meet, a "front" is produced. Fronts are where all the activity happens as the two air masses struggle with each other—their arrival and intensity announced by the cloud development that accompanies them. The

"...And there's only a slight chance of scattered flurries, nothing to worry about. Back to you Jim."

more extreme the difference is between the colliding masses, the more exciting the weather.

● Air pressure (measured with a barometer) is the weight of the air on the earth. One square inch (6.5 cm^2) column of still air that rises from sea level to the top of the atmosphere weighs 14.7 pounds (6.6 kg)—that's about as heavy as a day's worth of homework packed in your backpack. But the air doesn't just sit in one place over the earth—it's constantly moving. Warm air masses are less dense, and therefore put less pressure on the earth

than cold, dense air masses. Tornados, hurricanes, and storms are low-pressure systems. The strong winds that accompany them are caused by air rushing from surrounding high-pressure areas to fill the space in the low-pressure area. When there's only a slight difference in air pressure between the two masses, you'll measure a gentle breeze with your anemometer, as air calmly moves from areas of high pressure to low pressure. The barometer reflects the degree of pressure being exerted by the air at any given moment. It's one of the fundamental tools meteorologists have used for predicting changes in the weather.

● Meteorologists use high-tech versions of the same basic instruments you created to predict and monitor the weather, but they also have planes, satellites, and computers to aid them in preparing long-term forecasts and tracking storms that are hundreds of miles away. Even with all of the technology that's available, the weather can still produce phenomena that baffle the best predictors. Check out these bizarre weather incidents:

▶The fastest wind speed ever recorded on earth was 231 mph (370 kph) on Mt. Washington in New Hampshire, USA.

▶A storm in 1986 dropped hailstones that weighed more than 2 pounds (.9 kg) on Bangladesh.

▶In 1953, green-glowing snow fell in California. Any flesh that the snow touched developed a "blistered, itching rash." The Atomic Energy Commission denied any connection to recent A-bomb tests nearby.

▶In 1969, 5 feet, 8 inches (1.7 m) of snow fell in Bessans, France, in 19 hours.

▶The Atacama Desert in Chile had no rainfall for 14 years.

▶A 3-year drought in Northern China killed between 9 and 13 million people (1876-1879).

▶The fastest tornado was 280 miles per hour (448 kph) in Texas, USA, in 1958.

▶In 24 hours, 148 tornadoes swept through the southern and midwestern United States in 1974.

▶The most rain in one minute is 1½ inches (3.8 cm) (Guadeloupe Island in the Caribbean, 1970).

▶In 1916, the temperature dropped 100 degrees (44 to -56°F [7 to -49°C]) in a 24-hour period in Montana, USA.

Making a Barometer

(see figure 1)

WHAT YOU NEED

▶**Scissors**

▶**Balloon**

▶**1 glass jar**

▶**Rubber band**

▶**Drinking straw**

▶**Tape**

▶**Ruler**

▶**Piece of white paper**

▶**Pencil**

INSTRUCTIONS

1. Cut a piece of rubber from the top of the jar. Secure the rubber around the neck of the jar with a rubber band.

2. Snip one end of the straw to make a point. Tape the other end of the straw to the center of the rubber piece that covers the jar.

3. Tape the ruler to the piece of paper lengthwise. Tape the paper to a wall, and place the jar barometer next to it so the pointer is just a hair away from the paper.

Figure 1

4. Three times each day, check the level of the pointer against the paper and make a mark. Use the ruler to compare the distances between the marks. Each time you check the barometer, record where the mark lines up with the ruler in your notebook.

Making a Wind Vane
(see figure 2)

WHAT YOU NEED

► **Thin, long nail**
► **Drinking straw**
► **Wood glue**
► **1-inch (2.5 cm) diameter metal washer**
► **1-inch (2.5 cm) diameter wood dowel, 2 feet (61 cm) long**
► **Hammer**
► **Scissors**
► **Index card**
► **Thin, bendable wire**
► **Compass**

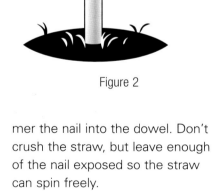

Figure 2

INSTRUCTIONS

1. Get an adult to help you make your wind vane. Carefully press the nail through the middle of the straw, so that the straw spins around the nail when you flick it.

2. Glue the washer, flat down to one end of the dowel.

3. Center the straw and nail over the circle in the washer, and ham-mer the nail into the dowel. Don't crush the straw, but leave enough of the nail exposed so the straw can spin freely.

4. Use the scissors to make 1-inch-long (2.5 cm) vertical slits in the top and bottom of the straw.

5. Slip the index card into the slit in the straw, and glue it in place. This end will catch the wind, and the other end of the straw will serve as the pointer.

6. Hold the dowel vertically, and center the wire horizontally across it, approximately 3 inches (7.6 cm) below the spinner.

7. Wrap the wire around the dowel to hold it in place (this should resemble a cross). Wrap the second piece of wire below the first in the same manner. Now you should have four arms of wire extending out from the dowel.

8. Bend the tip of each wire in the shape of a letter for one of the four directions, North, South, East, West. Be sure to follow the order of the directions.

9. Stick the bottom of the dowel in a planter or in the ground, and rotate it as needed so the directions of the wires point in the same directions as the compass.

10. To read the wind direction, just note the direction the pointer end of the weather vane faces. The wind will push the index card away from it, so the pointer end will tell you where the wind is coming from. If the pointer lines up between the direction wires, then record your wind as a northeast, southeast, southwest, or northwest.

Sticky Science

Satisfy your youthful curiosity about glue with this gooey experiment that tests the strength of a glue made out of milk and vinegar.

PROBLEM/PURPOSE

How does the strength of homemade glue compare to the strength of store-bought craft glue?

EXPERIMENT SUMMARY

Using milk, vinegar, and baking soda you'll make your own glue and then do a strength test against a name-brand craft glue.

WHAT YOU NEED

- Glass measuring cup
- Nonfat or lowfat milk
- Measuring spoon
- White vinegar
- Use of a microwave
- Scissors
- Coffee filter
- Funnel
- Plastic cup
- Baking soda
- Ruler
- Pen
- 12 wooden craft sticks
- 6 cotton swabs
- Name-brand white craft glue
- Stack of books
- 500 g x 10 g weight set*

You may be able to borrow one from your science teacher or buy it from a science supply catalog.

EXPERIMENTAL PROCEDURE

1. Pour ½ cup (120 mL) of nonfat or lowfat milk into the glass measuring cup.

2. Add 2 tablespoons (30 mL) of white vinegar to the milk and stir.

3. Microwave the solution for 20 to 30 seconds or until curdling occurs.

4. Trim the coffee filter with the scissors until it fits smoothly into the funnel.

5. Place the funnel over the plastic cup.

6. Pour the milk solution into the funnel until all the liquid drains. (You may need to let it drain for 10 to 15 minutes before proceeding with step 7.)

7. Pour out the liquid (this is called whey), and thoroughly rinse and dry the cup.

8. Scoop the curds from the filter into the cup. Discard the filter.

9. Add ¾ teaspoon (4 mL) of baking soda to the curds and mix well.

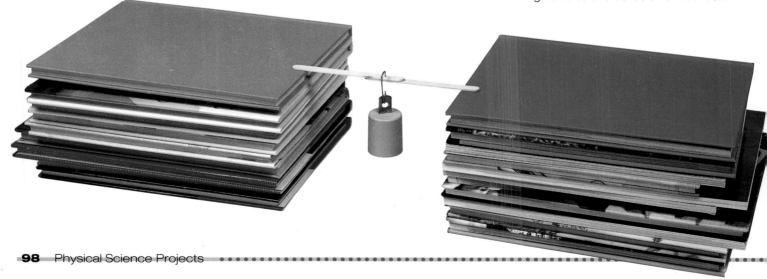

This will bubble and then produce a paste-like substance. There's your glue!

10. Measure 1 inch (2.5 cm) from the end of two wooden craft sticks and mark a line with the pen.

11. Measure ⅛ teaspoon (.6 mL) of your homemade paste. Using a cotton swab, spread this amount onto the end of one wooden craft stick. Discard the cotton swab.

12. Place the end of a second stick directly on top of the other so that the pen marks are overlapping. Let it dry overnight.

13. Repeat steps 11 and 12 using the name-brand white glue.

14. The next day, once the two bridges are dry, set up two equally thick book stacks directly across from each other on a table or desktop. Place your homemade glue bridge on top of them, spanning the area in between.

15. Place the books far enough apart so that the bridge is balancing with exactly one inch on each side. You'll need to use your ruler to check this!

16. Beginning with the 10 g weight, carefully add weight to the joint where you've glued the bridge. Wait one minute. Record your observations.

17. Continue adding weights, waiting one minute, and recording your observations with each new mass until the bridge breaks.

18. Repeat the strength test with the name-brand glued bridge.

19. Repeat the entire experiment (steps 11 through 18) three times.

CONCLUSION

Which bridge could withstand the most weight? Did the homemade-glued bridges work equally as well as the name brand glued ones? Can you recommend which glue would be strongest for attaching wood to wood? Display your results in a bar graph.

TAKE A CLOSER LOOK

● There are many different ingredients used to make glue. Most formulas contain *polymers*, which are large molecules made up of smaller ones in a strand. Some polymers are naturally "sticky," and others require ingredients to make them that way. The strength of the glue is determined by the attachment of the polymer to the surface of the item to be glued.

● Milk solids, or curds, are separated from the liquid by the vinegar. The curds dry to form a hard plastic-like substance called *casein*, which acts like an adhesive. The baking soda neutralizes any acid that's left in the milk. The resulting product is casein glue.

● Casein has been used for centuries in artists' paints as a means of adhering the paint to the canvas.

● Sticky trivia:

▶ The ancient Romans used beeswax and pine tar as a waterproof adhesive for shipbuilding.

▶ There's less than one-tenth of a calorie in the glue on the back of a stamp.

▶ The glue used to hold cigarettes together is made of casein (milk) and wax.

▶ The Aztec Indians used animal blood and cement as mortar for their buildings. Many of these buildings still stand today.

▶ Starch-based adhesives have been used for centuries. However, starch has no adhesive qualities until you boil it in water. It's commonly used in the production of paper as a binder and to control the ink penetration into the paper. Many cheaply made papers, such as newspaper, use less starch, which is why the ink rubs off on your hands.

▶ Hair spray, which is really a glue for hair, is made from *cellulose*, a protein in plant cell walls.

WHAT ELSE YOU CAN DO

● Perform the same type of test using your recommended glue with different materials, such as paper, metal, or plastic, to see which materials are best held together with the glue.

● Do the experiment using casein glue made from different types of milk: heavy cream, 2 percent, skim, and whole to see which is the strongest.

Outsmarting Hercules

You don't need the strength of Hercules to lift massive weights over your head, as long as you exercise some creative muscle. With a simple machine made from pulleys and ropes, you'll turn the impossible into a reality. Discover how many pulleys you need to make a device that will allow you to lift more weight than you could manage on your own.

PROBLEM/PURPOSE

How do pulleys work, and how many pulleys are needed to lift 100 pounds (45 kg)?

EXPERIMENT SUMMARY

You'll design a system of pulleys to see if it'll allow you to lift 100 pounds (45 kg) off the ground.

WHAT YOU NEED

▶ **2 sandbags, 50 pounds (22.7 kg) each**
▶ **5 pulleys**
▶ **Nylon rope**
▶ **Use of a doorway or other supportive beam structure**
▶ **Meterstick**
▶ **An adult assistant**

EXPERIMENTAL PROCEDURE

1. Choose a supportive door frame or the beam structure under a porch to set up the pulley system.

2. Have an adult locate the center of the top beam in the frame and screw three pulleys in place side-by-side. The wheels should turn parallel with the direction of the beam (see illustration below).

3. Screw the remaining two pulleys to one of the upright beams in the door frame, 1 foot (30.5 cm) from the floor. Place the pulleys side by side so the wheels spin parallel with the direction of the beam.

4. Tape a meterstick to the other upright beam in the door frame so that "0" is at the floor.

5. Place the sandbags under the top three pulleys, and securely tie

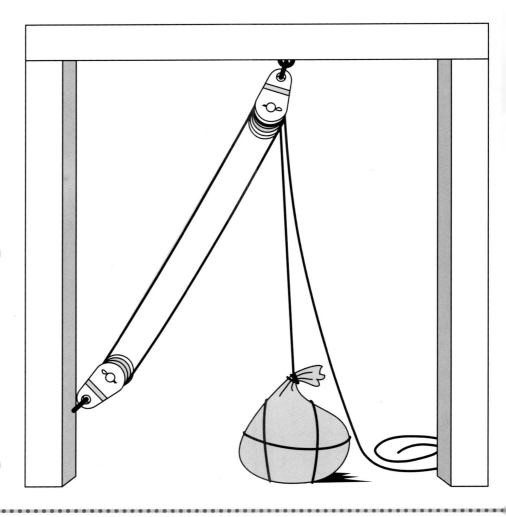

Cranes utilize pulleys to lift incredibly heavy objects.

the rope around the bags (ask your adult to assist you).

6. Run the other end of the rope over the first pulley above the bags, and pull the rope until it is taut between the bags and the pulleys.

7. Pull on the rope and attempt to lift the bags off the ground. Have your adult assistant watch the bottom of the bags and measure them against the meterstick on the door frame. Record the distance (if any) that you were able to lift the bags off the ground.

8. Thread the end of the rope through one of the bottom pulleys, and pull. Measure and record the height from the bottom of the bags to the ground.

9. Thread the rope from the bottom pulley up and through the center pulley in the block on the top beam. Make sure the ropes do not cross as they run between the pulleys.

10. Once again, try to lift the sandbags off the ground, now with the assistance of three pulleys. Record the distance you were able to lift the bags.

11. Continue to thread the rope between the pulleys, testing the effect of each one on the distance you can lift the bags. Be sure to record the distance (height from the bottom of the bags to the ground) after each lift attempt, noting the number of pulleys used.

CONCLUSION

Examine the distances for each lift attempt. How does using one pulley compare to using three? What is the effect of more pulleys on the time it takes to move the bags the same distance as with fewer pulleys?

TAKE A CLOSER LOOK

● If you were to lift your 100 pounds (45 kg) of material by simply attaching a rope to it, you'd need 100 pounds (45 kg) of force to lift it. Adding two pulleys, however, halves the amount of force needed to lift the weight. The weight is now supported by two ropes, each which hold half of the weight. So, if you want to lift the weight, you now only have to produce 50 pounds (22.7 kg) of force. The beam exerts the other 50 pounds (22.7 kg) of force on the other end of the rope. And adding more pulleys only helps matters more!

● Imagine that you're mountain climbing, and you're stranded in the middle of a huge rock face. You're attached to the wall securely, but you need food, water, and shelter from the winter storm that's building on the horizon. All of your supplies are in a huge bag, dangling at the end of a rope. No matter how hard you try, you can't pull up the rope because it's too heavy. Climbers who climb big walls face this challenge all the time. How do they deal with it? Simple, they use pulleys! Pulleys and ropes combine to form simple machines that help climbers haul all that weight.

DISPLAY TIPS

● Make a miniature model of the pulley system you used.

Wind Power!

What if you could harness the energy of the wind that blows around your home? Imagine powering a lightbulb, CD player, television, or video game without the electric company and the pollution that's created by burning fossil fuels. With this experiment, you'll determine whether or not you can use wind energy as a power source in your area.

A wind turbine in action

PROBLEM/PURPOSE

What is the average wind speed around your home?

EXPERIMENT SUMMARY

You'll make a simple anemometer to measure the wind speed around your home. Based on the average wind speed you record, you'll then determine whether or not wind energy would be a viable option.

WHAT YOU NEED

▶ **Anemometer (instructions to build one appear on page 104)**
▶ **Wristwatch**
▶ **Partner**

EXPERIMENTAL PROCEDURE

1. After assembling your anemometer, take a walk around the outside of your home and observe open areas where wind passes through. Look for a location that seems to get the most wind throughout the day. You'll probably find more wind as you move higher and farther from your home. If the homes in your neighborhood are close together, then look for wind tunnels—corridors between houses or buildings that tend to concentrate wind. If you have a flat roof or deck, ask an adult to check the wind level up there. Place the anemometer in the windiest location you can find.

2. Check the wind speed using your anemometer three times each day for 14 days. Stick to the same times in the morning, late afternoon, and evening for the entire experiment. Keep a chart to record the date, time, and wind speed for each observation. To determine wind speed, see Measuring and Calculating Wind Speed on page 104.

3. In addition to recording the wind speed from your anemometer, you should also record the general weather conditions at the time of each observation. This will help put your wind speed data into a context. For example, if a storm rolls over your area, you may get unusually high wind speeds that would lead to a higher average wind speed overall than normal. The Beaufort Scale (developed in 1806 by Admiral Sir Francis Beaufort) is a visual reference for estimating wind speed based on the reaction of objects to the wind. It's still used today for estimating wind speed (see page 103).

CONCLUSION

Examine your data from the 14 days of observation and calculate the average wind speed for each time of day. What time of the day is the windiest? When is it the calmest? Look at your visual weather observations and determine if there were any unusual weather events that may have influenced the wind speed. You should highlight these events in your journal and note them as variables. A small wind turbine for home use requires a minimum wind speed of 8 mph (12.8 kph) to operate. An average wind speed of 13 mph (20.8 kph) is recommended for economic efficiency. With this information, take a look at your data and ask whether a wind turbine could operate efficiently in your area or not.

TAKE A CLOSER LOOK

● From 7th-century Persia to 17th-century Holland, wind has been used to power windmills to pump water from wells, grind flour, and irrigate fields. But it wasn't until the 1800s that the windmill was used to directly produce electricity. Compared to the wooden windmills we're familiar with in history books and paintings, today's "wind turbines" are high-tech machines made of metal and controlled by computers. In fact, some wind turbines are giants with blades that stretch 65 meters to their tips and stand 100 meters tall! Used alone to generate power for small communities, or combined with others to form entire "wind farms," there are more than 40,000 wind turbines spinning their steel arms to produce energy in 40 countries from New Zealand and India to Germany and the United States.

● Compared to coal and oil as fuels, wind power still lags behind, producing less than 1 percent of the world's electricity. But with continued improvements to wind turbines, they could become part of a group of cleaner and renewable energy technologies, including solar, that can replace traditional nonrenewable energy sources. Coal, for example, is the number one source of energy in the world, but it comes with a cost. Burning coal releases carbon dioxide, a greenhouse gas associated with global warming, and sulphur dioxide, which contributes to acid rain. Scientists, environmentalists, and engineers look to wind energy, which doesn't directly produce air pollution and is naturally available for use all over the world, as a healthier alternative for the planet.

BEAUFORT SCALE

Beaufort #	Mph/Kph	Conditions
LIGHT WINDS		
0	1 (1.6)	smoke rises straight up
1	1–3 (1.6–4.8)	smoke drifts slowly
2	4–7 (6.4–11.2)	wind vane moves and wind lightly rustles leaves
3	8–12 (12.8–19.2)	dust rises, leaves and twigs move
MODERATE WINDS		
4	13–18 (20.8–28.8)	small branches move, dust blows
5	19–24 (30.4–38.4)	small trees sway
STRONG WINDS		
6	25–31 (40–49.6)	large branches move, umbrellas become difficult to use
7	32–38 (51.2–60.8)	trees in motion, walking is slightly difficult
GALE FORCE WINDS		
8	39–46 (62.4–73.6)	twigs break off trees
9	47–54 (75.2–86.4)	branches break off trees, slight damage to buildings
10	55–63 (88–100.8)	small trees uprooted, definite building damage
STORM FORCE WINDS		
11	64–74 (102.4–118.4)	widespread damage
HURRICANE WINDS		
12	75–plus (120)	extreme damage

Building the Anemometer

WHAT YOU NEED

- ▶ 2 inch x 2 inch x 4-foot (5.1 x 5.1 x 122 cm) piece of wood (A)
- ▶ 1 x 1-foot (30.5 x 30.5 cm) block of wood, 3/4 inch (1.9 cm) thick (B)
- ▶ Hammer
- ▶ 2 nails, 1½ inches (3.8 cm) long
- ▶ Pencil or pen
- ▶ Drill with ¼-inch (6 mm) bit
- ▶ Scissors
- ▶ Drinking straw
- ▶ ⅝-inch (1.6 cm) metal washer
- ▶ Wood glue
- ▶ 2 pieces of wood trim, ½ inch x 1 inch x 2 feet (1.3 x 2.5 x 61 cm) (C)
- ▶ Vegetable oil
- ▶ 4 yogurt cups
- ▶ Acrylic paint
- ▶ Paintbrush
- ▶ 4 tacks

INSTRUCTIONS

1. Get an adult to help you make your anemometer. Stand the 2 inch x 2 inch x 4-foot (5.1 x 5.1 x 122 cm) (A) piece of wood on one end, and center the wood block (B) on top of it. Have an adult help you hammer one of the nails through the center of the block into the end of the piece of wood (see illustration). This will be the stand for the anemometer.

2. Flip the stand around so the wood block is on the ground, and mark a dot in the center of the end of the wood.

3. Have an adult drill a 2-inch-deep (5.1 cm) hole into the stand where you marked the dot.

4. Cut a piece from the drinking straw to fit inside of the drilled hole. Insert the piece of straw all the way into the hole so that the top end is level with the top of the hole.

5. Line up the hole in the washer with the hole in the wood, and glue the washer in place.

6. Take the two pieces of wood trim (C) and make a cross. Hammer the remaining nail straight through the center of the cross.

7. Center the cross horizontally over the hole in the stand so the sharp end of the nail fits inside the hole. Give the cross a whirl to see if it spins smoothly. You may want to rub vegetable oil on the washer to reduce friction between the parts.

8. Paint the outside of one of the yogurt cups with the acrylic paint, and let it dry.

9. Tack the side of a yogurt cup to one of the cross ends, as shown in the illustration. Use glue between the cup and the wood for reinforcement in addition to the tack. Glue and tack the remaining cups to each of the ends of the cross so that the open ends of the cups face the same direction.

MEASURING AND CALCULATING WIND SPEED

1. Ask your partner to time you for one minute as you count the number of times the colored yogurt cup makes a complete circle. Record this number as X revolutions per minute (rpm).

2. Next, find the circumference of the anemometer (the distance around the circle of yogurt cups): circumference = 3.14 (pi) x diameter (the distance across the center of the circle). The circumference calculated for the illustrated anemometer is 6.3 feet (1.9 m) (3.14 x 2 feet [61 cm] = 6.28 feet [1.9 m]).

3. Multiply the circumference by the revolutions per minute (X rpm) to get the wind speed in feet per minute.

4. Convert the wind speed from feet per minute to miles per hour by multiplying the wind speed by .0114: x ft /min. (.0114) = X miles /hr. Convert mph to kph by multiplying by 1.6.

Take a Closer Look:
The Daring Divas of Science

Open a book on famous discoveries in science, and you'll find plenty of references to famous inventors and scientists with names like Otto, William, John, and Sir So-and-So, but where are the women? You almost need a magnifying glass to find them. Nevertheless, throughout history women have made major contributions to science—sometimes risking their lives in pursuit of their scientific goals. Here are just a few of the many women who struggled to study and practice science:

Agnodice (300 B.C.E.) had to dress as a man in order to study medicine in Athens, Greece. She was nearly put to death when her gender was discovered.

Miriam the Prophetess (1st c. C.E.) laid down the theoretical and practical basis of Western Alchemy, and thus of modern chemistry. She invented laboratory equipment for sublimation and distillation, and her *balneum mariae* (water bath) has remained essential laboratory equipment for almost 2,000 years.

Hypatia (370–415 C.E.) was a teacher of mathematics and natural philosophy in Alexandria, Egypt. She also invented the astrolabe, the planisphere, a distillation device, and the hydrometer. She was brutally murdered by a mob raised up by Roman politicians and religious leaders who believed her outspokenness was a threat to their authority.

Trotula of Salerno (?–1097 C.E.) practiced medicine in southern Italy. She wrote one of the first medical guides for women and physicians of the medieval era.

Maria Sibylle Merian (1647–1717) was one of the first women entomologists, and her books became reference guides for future generations of insect lovers.

Lady Mary Wortley Montagu (1689–1762) introduced cowpox inoculations to Europe. Smallpox had killed more than 60 million people before Lady Montagu's injections put an end to this disease. Her work laid the groundwork for the germ theory of diseases. (An interesting side note: historians think that the inoculation against smallpox was probably first discovered by milk maids, whose exposure to cowpox made them immune to smallpox.)

Caroline Herschel (1750–1848) founded sidereal astronomy (the study of star systems), and discovered 8 comets and 17 nebulae. In 1787, she was given a 50-pound annual salary for her position as Assistant Court Astronomer, the same job her brother earned 200 pounds a year to do.

Ada Byron Lovelace (1815–1852) predicted the uses and limitations of computers and the first programs for their use. She also made clear the basis for modern computer programming. The U.S. Navy named a computer language after her.

Marie Sklodowska Curie (1867–1934) twice won the Nobel Prize for her work with radioactive elements. She isolated pure radium, and with Henri Becquerel and her husband, Pierre Curie, discovered radium and polonium.

Lise Meitner (1878–1968) theorized that atoms could be split apart to release energy—the foundation of nuclear energy. Lise discovered the element *protactinium* in 1918 with her lab partner Otto Hahn. A nobel prize was awarded to Otto Hahn, but not to Lise, for the discovery.

Rachel Carson (1907–1964) wrote extensively on the subject of nature. Her observations contributed heavily to the foundation of modern ecology.

Rosalind Elsie Franklin (1920–1957) is credited with first recognizing the helix shape of DNA.

Katsuko Saruhushi (1920–) studied carbon dioxide in the environment long before people started to worry about the greenhouse effect. She also measured the radioactivity of seawater following the first hydrogen bomb tests.

Dueling Densities

Liquid motion lamps, those colorful bubbling throwbacks from the 1960s, turn liquids of different densities into a fascinating display. With some patience and a careful hand, you can make your own lamp for hours of psychedelic fun.

PROBLEM/PURPOSE

What's the proper ratio of two or more liquids of different densities that'll cause the "lava" to float in a liquid motion lamp?

EXPERIMENTAL SUMMARY

You and an adult will mix liquids of different densities in a bottle, and find the proper ratio that'll produce the dancing effect seen in a liquid motion lamp.

WHAT YOU NEED

▸ **20-ounce (600 mL) glass bottle**
▸ **Tin snips**
▸ **Medium-sized coffee can**
▸ **Lamp base and 40-watt light bulb (this is the maximum recommended wattage for this experiment)**
▸ **2 ounces (60 mL) or more mineral oil**
▸ **5 ounces (150 mL) or more of 90-percent isopropyl alcohol** CVS
▸ **13 ounces (390 mL) or more of 70-percent isopropyl alcohol**
▸ **Food coloring (color of choice)**

EXPERIMENTAL PROCEDURE

1. Rinse the glass bottle and let it dry. Peel off all labels from the bottle.

2. Use the tin snips to cut a hole in the bottom of the coffee can. The hole should be slightly smaller than the bottom of the glass bottle so that the bottle will be able to sit over the hole without falling through it.

3. At the top rim of the coffee can, cut a 1-inch (2.5 cm) slot large enough for the lamp cord to pass through.

4. Turn the coffee can upside down over the lamp base and lightbulb. The lightbulb should be centered under the hole in the base of the coffee can.

5. Feed the lamp cord through the small slot you made near the rim of the can. Place the bottle upright on top of the can, over the lightbulb hole.

6. Pour 2 ounces (60 mL) of mineral oil into the bottom of the bottle, then pour 5 ounces (150 mL) of 90-percent isopropyl alcohol into the bottle. Let the liquids settle. Record your observations.

7. Add a few drops of food coloring to the mixture, and turn the lamp on. Warning! The glass bottle will get quite hot while you're performing this experiment.

8. Slowly add the 70-percent isopropyl alcohol to the bottle. Let the contents mix and settle every 2 ounces (60 mL). The objective is to add enough of the 70-percent alcohol to the mixture to cause the mineral oil to become suspended and dance in the bottle. As you get close to this point, the mineral oil will turn whitish and begin to look more and more like the "lava" you're used to seeing in the store-bought lamps. Record what happens after each addition of alcohol. Warning! Don't leave this lamp unattended while it's on.

CONCLUSION

What happened when you added the 90-percent alcohol to the mineral oil? What happened each time you added the 70-percent alcohol to the mixture? In the end, how many ounces of each substance did you need to produce the effects you wanted? How did the liquids respond to the heat under the bottle? What happened to the mixture after you turned the lamp off?

TAKE A CLOSER LOOK

● Two or more liquids of different densities combined in a mixture will eventually settle out by their weight. The heaviest liquid will sit on the bottom of the bottle and the lightest liquid will float on top. When heat is introduced under the bottle, the contents warm, and the dense bottom liquid expands, becomes lighter, and rises. If the top substance is close in density to the bottom liquid, then the bottom

liquid may become light enough to displace the top liquid. This is the dance you observe in the liquid motion lamp.

● Oil and water have different densities, but don't work in this experiment because there is too great a difference between the densities of the two substances. By the time the water expands and becomes light enough to reach the density of the oil, the oil has warmed up, expanded, and become even lighter.

● Density is a reflection of how tightly packed the molecules of a particular substance are—it's the weight-per-unit volume of a substance. The more tightly packed the molecules, the more dense the substance.

WHAT ELSE YOU CAN DO

● Try mixing other liquids that have slightly different densities in the bottle to see if you can achieve a similar effect. Try combining some of the following ingredients: vegetable oils, water, salt water, honey, glycerine, dish soap, or castor oil.

● You can experiment with the lamp's color by using a few drops of oil-based paint, or chopping up the contents of a permanent-ink marker and adding the colored pulp to the lamp.

Chemistry
THE SCIENCE OF FORMS OF MATTER

HOUSEHOLD
CLEANERS

SALT

DYES

CHLORINE

pH

RUST

CO^2

AND MUCH, MUCH MORE!

I'm Dyeing to Find Out

Dyes are materials that give color to paper, cloth, and yarn. Though most dyes today are synthetic (made artificially), people have been dyeing with natural materials for thousands of years, using leaves, flowers, roots, bark, nutshells, weeds, vegetables, fruits, minerals, shellfish, and even bugs. Here's a simple way to see just how well natural dyeing works.

?

PROBLEM/PURPOSE

Which vegetables make the best dye?

EXPERIMENT SUMMARY

You'll boil three vegetables to see which will produce the deepest color on a strip of a white T-shirt.

WHAT YOU NEED

- **Protective goggles**
- **Smock**
- **Measuring cup**
- **A parent to assist**
- **Knife**
- **6 cups red onion skins**
- **Old saucepan (it will probably get stained)**
- **Water**
- **Use of a stove**
- **Potato masher**
- **Rubber gloves**
- **Wooden spoon**
- **9 white cotton fabric strips (tear up an old T-shirt)**
- **Tray**
- **Paper towels**
- **Masking tape**
- **Permanent marker**
- **6 cups beet slices**
- **6 cups purple cabbage skins**

EXPERIMENTAL PROCEDURE

1. Put on the protective goggles and smock. Have a parent help chop the 6 cups of onion skins finely.

2. Put the onion skins in the old saucepan with enough water to cover the skins.

3. Heat the skins on the stove until the water boils. Turn down the heat and simmer.

4. After 10 minutes, use the potato masher to mash the

skins even further to help the juice come out.

5. Simmer for 35 to 45 minutes longer, or until the liquid in the pot is dark. Add extra water if the mixture gets too dry.

6. Put on your gloves, and add three T-shirt strips to the mixture and stir for 5 minutes with the spoon. Let the strips sit in the mixture for 30 minutes.

7. Lay several layers of paper towels over the tray, and use the masking tape and permanent marker to label the towel where you'll place the strips.

8. Remove the strips with the spoon, and place them on the tray

where you've labeled the towel layer. Allow the strips to dry.

9. Wash the saucepan, potato masher, and spoon thoroughly.

10. Repeat steps 1 through 9 for the beets and then the cabbage.

11. Once the fabric strips are all dry, compare the colors, and write down your observations.

CONCLUSION

Which vegetable gave you the deepest, darkest color? Was it as deep as you thought it would be? What other vegetables do you think would provide good color? The best way to record your results is to comment on your personal observations. Check the colors and decide whether or not any of the strips look faded or not very colorful. Compare the strips to the

remains of the white T-shirt you used to make the strips.

TAKE A CLOSER LOOK

● When fabrics are dyed, the dye molecules are attaching themselves onto the fabric's fibers.

● Plants contain many pigments for photosynthesis—some we can see and some we can't. These pigments are found in the leaves, bark, berries, and fruit of plants.

WHAT ELSE YOU CAN DO

● Try dyeing with other vegetables, weeds, nuts, and flowers to see which produce good colors.

● To create a fabric color that's truly colorfast (that won't run or fade), you'll need to pretreat the fabric with a *mordant* (an agent that fixes dyes to materials). Research the different mordants available and compare their effectiveness.

● Compare fabrics that have been pretreated with a mordant with fabrics that haven't been pretreated with one. Put the fabrics in the sun for several days. Does the mordant make a difference in how long the color lasts?

DISPLAY TIPS

● Bring a sample of the vegetables you used along with your dyed fabric, and place the fabric next to the vegetable you used to dye it.

Enzymes in Action

Enzymes are large proteins with unique shapes, sort of like puzzle pieces. Living things use enzymes as catalysts to make things happen quickly that otherwise would happen very, very slowly. If an enzyme loses its unique shape, it can't do its job—the same way you couldn't build a puzzle if the edges of the pieces had been removed. How does changing the pH affect the enzymes of an apple and a potato?

PROBLEM/PURPOSE

What does it take to change an enzyme's shape? (And what the heck is an enzyme, anyway?)

EXPERIMENTAL SUMMARY

In this experiment, you'll try to change the enzyme responsible for fruit and vegetable turning brown. When you cut a piece of fruit, such as an apple, you bring the enzyme *catecholase* into contact with other molecules, which starts the browning process. If you change the enzyme's shape, the molecules can't fit together. You'll attempt to change the enzyme's shape by changing the pH of the fruit (which is a measure of the fruit's acidity or basicity).

WHAT YOU NEED

► 3 apples
► Vegetable peeler
► Stopwatch
► 3 potatoes
► pH test kit*
► Lemon juice (fresh-squeezed or bottled)
► Table salt
► Cup
► Water
► Spoon (to mix salt in water)

*Available at science supply stores and some school supply stores (ask your teacher if you're having trouble finding one)

EXPERIMENTAL PROCEDURE

1. To set up your controls, carefully remove the skin from part of an apple with the peeler.

2. Watch the apple, and record how long it takes for the fruit to begin turning brown.

3. Repeat with a potato.

4. Use a pH kit to test the acidity of your lemon juice. Record the pH number.

5. Peel part of another apple, and immediately cover the peeled fruit with lemon juice.

6. Record how long it takes for the apple to brown. Stop counting if it hasn't turned brown within 20 minutes.

7. Repeat with a second potato.

8. Dissolve as much table salt as possible in a cup of water, and use the pH kit to test the acidity of the salty water. Record the pH number.

9. Peel part of a third apple, and immediately cover the peeled fruit with the salty water.

10. Record how long it takes for the apple to brown. Stop counting if it hasn't turned brown within 20 minutes.

11. Repeat with a third potato.

CONCLUSION

Look at your results and compare them to the control. Did the lemon juice stop the browning? If so, that means the pH was acidic enough to change the shape of the enzyme. If not, try to find something more acidic than lemon juice and repeat the experiment. Ask the same questions about the salt water. What could you do if you wanted to keep the peeled apples in a fruit salad from turning brown? Record your results in a table.

TAKE A CLOSER LOOK

● Enzymes work best at a neutral pH (7.0). Conditions that are too acidic (low pH) or too basic (high pH) prevent the enzyme from functioning by changing its shape, rendering it unable to do its job.

● Another way to easily change an enzyme's shape is to expose it to a high temperature. (Have you ever wondered why parents flip out over high fevers? If your body temperature goes too high, the thousands of enzymes in your body begin to lose their shape, which can cause lots of problems.)

WHAT ELSE YOU CAN DO

● Repeat the experiments with solutions that have pH values between the lemon juice and the salt water. Try to determine the minimum and maximum pH values needed to change the enzymes' shapes.

DISPLAY TIPS

● Exhibit samples or photographs of the apples or potatoes with the different solutions on them.

"Take your time with your science fair project. Don't rush, even if your due date is soon. Even if you don't completely finish, be proud of what you did."
—Julie Ann Olbrantz, 7th grader

"Doing a project for a science fair was a wonderful experience. One piece of advice: make your project eye-catching. It makes the project more interesting to look at, and the judges love stuff like that."
—Alex Fisher, 8th grader

Exercise Your Rights to Produce CO_2

When you run, ride, or otherwise expend energy, you exhale carbon dioxide as a result of cellular respiration. When carbon dioxide *(CO₂)* mixes with water, it produces *carbonic acid* (the same stuff that makes your cola fizzy!). This experiment provides a pHantastic way to see how exercise affects the amount of *CO₂* produced.

PROBLEM/PURPOSE

What effects do different types of exercise have on the production of carbon dioxide in humans?

EXPERIMENT SUMMARY

After various types of exercise, you'll have volunteers blow into a cup of water. You'll then measure its pH to see if the carbonic acid level increases or stays the same.

WHAT YOU NEED

▶ **At least 10 volunteers (the more the better)**
▶ **Plastic cup for each volunteer**
▶ **Tap water**
▶ **Watch**
▶ **Drinking straw (1 for each volunteer)**
▶ **pH paper***

*Can be purchased from a science supply catalog, or ask your science teacher for the best place to obtain it

EXPERIMENTAL PROCEDURE

1. Fill the plastic cup with 8 ounces (240 mL) of tap water.

2. Measure the pH of the water, and record it in a table in your notebook.

3. Your first volunteer should then blow into the cup of water with the straw for 30 seconds.

4. Test the pH of the water immediately after the 30 seconds with the pH paper. Compare the color of the paper with the color on the standards (usually on the outside of the container), and record the pH of the water in the table.

5. Pour out the water and fill the cup with 8 ounces (240 mL) of fresh water.

6. Now you're ready to begin the experimental portion of the test.

7. Have your first volunteer run in place for five minutes. Repeat steps 3 through 5.

8. Have the volunteer rest for two minutes, then have him perform 25 sit-ups. Repeat steps 3 through 5.

9. Have the volunteer rest for two minutes and then do 10 push-ups. Repeat steps 3 through 5.

10. Have the volunteer rest for two more minutes and then do 20 military presses. To perform a military press, the volunteer should:

A) Reach above his head with his arms and then touch his waist with his hands.

B) Reach down to his toes.

C) Place his hands on the ground, bend his knees, and shoot out his legs behind him until they're fully

extended, toes touching the ground.

D) Bring his legs back into a crouched position.

E) Stand up and repeat! (Isn't this FUN!?)

11. Repeat steps 3 and 4.

12. Repeat the experiment with the rest of the volunteers.

CONCLUSION

Compare the pH levels of the water for each volunteer before the experiment and after each exercise. Was there a difference in pH before and after the exercises? Did any one exercise cause a noticeable drop in pH? Did the pH decrease with more exercise or remain the same? Compare the lowest pH levels of all the volunteers. Average the volunteers' pH levels after each exercise and before exercising, and display this on a bar graph.

TAKE A CLOSER LOOK

● pH is a measure of the amount of hydrogen ions in a solution. It measures the acidity or basicity of a solution. When you exhale CO_2 and blow into the water, the solution will turn more acidic due to an increase in carbonic acid.

● The pH of an acid is less than 7, with 1 being the most acidic. When you exercise, your cells use a chemical called ATP *(adenosine triphosphate)* to produce energy. During the process of "burning" ATP, your muscles need oxygen, and they need to get rid of the waste products produced. These include CO_2, heat, and *lactic acid* (lactic acid is the stuff that makes your muscles feel sore and achy). CO_2 is then carried out of the muscle cells by the blood. The blood goes to your lungs and is exchanged with more oxygen you're breathing in. You, of course, then exhale the CO_2.

Bubblerama!

Here's a chance to do some serious science and play with bubbles at the same time. Bubbles are a lot of fun, and this experiment tests the best conditions for long-lasting bubbles.

PROBLEM/PURPOSE

How does temperature affect the life span of a bubble?

EXPERIMENT SUMMARY

You'll blow bubbles in a clear jar and then place the jar in different temperatures to test which temperature provides for the longest-lasting bubbles.

WHAT YOU NEED

► **Clear jar or glass**
► **Water**
► **Measuring spoons**
► **Bubble solution**
► **Thermometer**
► **Drinking straw**
► **Stopwatch**
► **Plastic wrap**

EXPERIMENTAL PROCEDURE

1. Wet the inside of your jar. Make sure the rim is also wet.

2. Place ½ teaspoon (2.5 mL) of bubble solution in the bottom of the jar.

3. Record the room temperature.

4. Wet the straw and blow into the jar, just above the bubble solution, until the jar is filled with bubbles (see demonstration photo). If you have too many or not enough bubbles, change the amount of solution in the jar and retest.

5. Once the jar is filled with bubbles, begin timing how long the

bubbles last. Quickly place the plastic wrap over the jar as you begin timing. You might want to have an assistant place the plastic over the jar as you begin the stopwatch.

6. Stop timing once the final bubble pops. Record the time.

7. Repeat steps 1 through 6 nine more times. Record the average of the 10 trials.

8. Repeat the experiment in the freezer, in the refrigerator, in direct sunlight, and possibly even in the oven (make sure you have adult supervision if you decide to do this, and don't use the plastic wrap for this or any of the other temperatures). Record the temperature in each location you choose. Since humidity also affects a bubble's life span, do the whole experiment in one day.

CONCLUSION

Once you've gotten your averages for each of the different temperatures, plot them on a line graph, with the x-axis the temperature and the y-axis the number of seconds the bubbles lasted. What was your optimum temperature?

TAKE A CLOSER LOOK

● At a higher temperature, the liquid film that contains the bubble will not be as thick, and so will thin out faster. Also, it'll evaporate faster, so the film will thin more rapidly to the point where it's no longer strong enough to resist popping. If, on the other hand, the temperature becomes too low, the soap might become less soluble in water to the point where there won't be enough soap molecules to form a good film. Also, the surface of the bubble might change when the temperature is lowered (to a more condensed state) leaving part of the surface uncovered, which leads to POP!

WHAT ELSE YOU CAN DO

● Since all liquids make bubbles, experiment with several to see which ones make the longest-lasting ones.

● Test the effect humidity has on bubbles.

Take a Closer Look:
Tables and Graphs

Tables and graphs not only look great on your display board, but they also present important information in a way that makes it easy to understand. Make sure to number your tables or graphs and give them titles.

Data tables (Table 1) are useful for recording and organizing your experimental results. Make sure to label all columns, and include units of measurement in the headings.

Here's a line graph (Graph 1) displaying the same information in the table. Line graphs are best used to show continuous data points relating to your independent variable. Patterns and trends are easily identified on a line graph so the reader can better understand your results.

Use a bar graph (Graph 2) to show separate and distinct groups in your data. For example, if you were just comparing average science test scores between classes, you could use a bar graph.

Also referred to as a circle graph, a pie chart (Graph 3) presents information in percentages. The whole circle equals 100 percent, and the different pieces of the pie make up different portions of the whole.

Table 1. Science Test Scores for Three Classes

Study Time (min.)	Average Science Test Score			
	Class 1	Class 2	Class 3	Average
0	45	55	35	45
20	60	64	70	64.7
30	65	65	80	70
40	72	80	84	78.7
50	82	88	93	87.7
60	90	95	99	94.7
60+	93	97	100	96.7

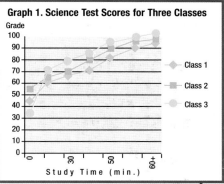

Graph 1. Science Test Scores for Three Classes

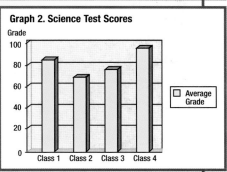

Graph 2. Science Test Scores

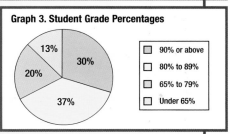

Graph 3. Student Grade Percentages

Chromatography: What's in a Color?

That pen may flow with blue ink, and that instant drink mix may look red, but both are actually mixtures of various chemical compounds. With paper chromatography, scientists can separate these mixtures into their pure elements. Like breaking a code, a chemist can then analyze the colored, chemical separation of a mixture and identify the components that make it unique.

PROBLEM/PURPOSE

What's the best solvent for separating out the elements of purple, red, and green markers, or of instant drink mix?

EXPERIMENT SUMMARY

You'll make and compare chromatographs using alcohol, water, vinegar, and ammonia as solvents to separate the components of colored markers or drink mix on filter paper.

WHAT YOU NEED

- Cone-shaped coffee filters
- Pencil
- Ruler
- 3 packages of drink mix colored purple, red, and green or 3 colored, water-based markers in purple, red, and green
- Dropper
- 12 clear plastic, 8-ounce (240 mL) cups or glass beakers
- Masking tape
- Isopropyl alcohol
- Vinegar
- Household ammonia (use extreme caution)
- Water
- 12 rubber bands
- 12 paper clips
- Paper towels

EXPERIMENTAL PROCEDURE

1. On each coffee filter, mark a point with the pencil ¾ inch (1.9 cm) from the tip of the cone on each side. Don't open up any of the filters, but leave them stuck together for this experiment.

2. Make another pencil mark ¾ inch (1.9 cm) down from the wide end on both sides of each filter cone.

3. Select a filter and a marker. With a pencil, write the color of the marker you've selected across the wide end of the cone above the mark you made in step 2. If using drink mix, label the cone with the color of the mix you're testing.

4. Make pea-sized dots with the marker on the pencil marks at the tip of the filter cone. For the drink mix, make a serving as directed on the package. Use a dropper to place one drop of the drink solution onto both marks at the tip of the filter cone. Allow the marker or drink mix solution to dry.

5. Repeat steps 3 and 4 for the remaining colored markers or mixes.

6. Separate the plastic cups into three groups of four. Use the tape and the pencil to label the cups in each group with the name of a different solvent: alcohol, water, vinegar, and ammonia. Measure and mark a line ½ inch (1.3 cm) from the bottom of each cup.

7. Carefully pour each solvent into its matching group of cups. Get an adult to help you with the solvents. Fill the cups just to the line you marked on each.

8. Stretch a rubber band across the mouth and over the bottom of each cup. Attach a paper clip to the rubber band so that the paper clip hangs down over the center of the cup's mouth.

9. Slowly and carefully slip the coffee filters into the cups so the pointed ends are in the solvent. The marker or drink mix dots should be just above the level of the solvent in the cups. Clip the wide end of each cone to the rubber band so that the sides of each filter don't touch the sides of the cups.

10. Let all of the cones sit in the cups until the water has climbed to the marks near the wide end of each cone. Remove each filter, open them up, and let them dry on a piece of paper towel.

CONCLUSION

Compare the patterns created on each filter. Did you notice that some solvents worked better than others at drawing out the separate colors from the original solution? Which separations took the longest and which took the shortest amount of time to complete? Are any of the chromatographs consistently the same color; in other words, is there little separation in the color as it is spread throughout the filter?

TAKE A CLOSER LOOK

● Chromatography is used by scientists in many fields to break down mixtures into their raw elements, identified by the color separations that result on the paper. These chemical elements are made up of molecules that have different degrees of affinity (an attraction for) the solvent, which in this experiment included water, alcohol, vinegar, and ammonia. Those molecules that have a strong affinity for water are called *hydrophilic* and will cling to the water molecules as they spread out and progress up the filter paper. The movement of water through the paper filter is based on capillary action—the same process plants use to move water through their stems and leaves. Some molecules are *hydrophobic*, meaning they are not soluble in water, and will respond better to other solvents such as alcohol. The size of the molecules also affects the distance that they will travel; essentially, the smaller the molecule, the farther it will go. Another factor that determines how the original solution separates out into its chemical components involves the affinity some molecules have for the support, which is the filter paper.

● Each line of separation in a chromatograph represents a different component of the original solution. The pattern that is created is like a fingerprint for identifying the original mixture. In fact, chromatography is used by police and forensics experts to identify criminals by breaking down the ink used in notes and letters and tracing the pattern to the criminal's pen. And chromatography is one technique used to spot drugs in urine. Biochemists and analytical chemists study chromatograph patterns to identify the chemicals that comprise a wide spectrum of mixtures from pollutants to perfumes and blood.

Fishing for Chlorine

Chlorine is the powerful compound we use to disinfect swimming pools, whiten towels, and clean kitchen items. But did you know that chlorine is also used to treat the wastewater from sewage treatments plants, and that this water may still contain chlorine when dumped into the nearest river? Go exploring with this experiment to collect water samples and test them for their chlorine content.

PROBLEM/PURPOSE

How much chlorine is in the river around a sewage treatment plant?

EXPERIMENTAL SUMMARY

Collect six samples of water from a river that flows by a sewage treatment plant, and compare the chlorine content of the upstream samples with those you collected downstream from the plant.

WHAT YOU NEED

► **6 glass jars with lids**
► **Chlorine test kit***
► **Rubber gloves**
► **An assistant**

* The kind used for checking the chlorine levels in pools

EXPERIMENTAL PROCEDURE

1. Contact your local sewage treatment plant or public works department and find out where the treatment plant discharges its treated effluent. You may be able to take a tour of your local facility and see how the whole sewage treatment process works (if you do, take pictures!). Find out where you can safely access the river to take water samples. The sewage plant staff may also have a copy of the guidelines they have to follow for the amount of chlorine they're allowed to use and discharge. Your state or province's department of natural resources or environmental protection agency should be able to tell you what they consider to be safe levels of chlorine in public waterways. You can also inquire at a pet store about the safe levels of chlorine for fish.

2. With the help of an adult, collect a jar of water from a calm, clear spot along the river's edge at these points:

► 1 mile (1.6 km) above and below the treatment plant

► ½ mile (.8 km) above and below the treatment plant

► 1 foot (30.5 cm) (or as close as you can get) before and after the treatment plant.

Be sure to label each jar with a letter that corresponds to its collection location, and record this in your notebook.

3. Follow the directions provided with your chlorine test kit to test each of the samples. Don't mix any of the water between the samples through the course of your tests.

4. Record your test results and compare them with the information you gathered about safe and unsafe chlorine levels.

CONCLUSION

Which sections of the river provided the highest and lowest chlorine levels? How does this relate to the location of the sewer treatment plant? Would the chlorine levels of your samples be safe for pet store fish? Are the chlorine levels safe according to government guidelines for your region?

TAKE A CLOSER LOOK

● Chlorine has many beneficial uses in modern life, and traces of it can be found in many familiar places. Look at this white sheet of paper you're reading. It was probably bleached with chlorine to remove the natural brown color of the wood so you could read these words more easily. Hospitals, schools, and other institutions rely on chlorine bleach to disinfect equipment and to remove stains from clothing, towels, and bedding. But just as chlorine is effective in killing harmful microorganisms, it's also deadly to other forms of life, including humans.

● If you have an aquarium, you probably already know to test the tap water for chlorine before you fill the tank with it. Too much chlorine can be harmful to fish and other aquarium life. Likewise, too much chlorine is toxic to the many forms of life that inhabit rivers. In fact, high concentrations of chlorine have been responsible for fish kills and loss of life in otherwise pristine streams and rivers. There's also a concern that chlorine reacts with other compounds when released into the environment and forms different toxic or potentially cancer-causing substances, such as chloroform and dioxin. Dioxin is particular-

ly nasty and a major concern of ecologists, because it's a toxic compound that's stored in the fat tissues of animals and passed on through the food chain to humans.

● You can take steps in your everyday life to reduce your use of chlorine, and thereby limit the amount you discard into the environment. For example, try using biodegradable or natural cleansers in your home; products made from citrus fruits are effective and smell much better than bleach. When given the option, buy non-chlorine bleached napkins, toilet paper, paper towels, computer paper, and notebook paper.

WHAT ELSE YOU CAN DO

● Observe how chlorine levels vary with rain and water levels by comparing six samples collected on a rainy day with six others collected on a sunny day.

● Compare the types of organisms you find living in areas where the chlorine concentration differs. Take a field guide, fish net, shallow pan, magnifying glass, and rubber

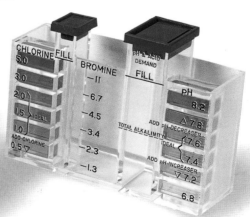

gloves down to the river bank and look for common invertebrates (such as insect larvae), crayfish, snails, and fish. Compare the types and sizes of organisms you find in the different locations, and compare them with the chlorine test results.

● You can also test the water quality of the river for other factors, such as pH, phosphorus, nitrogen, ammonia, and pesticides. Many of the test kits for these substances can be found in the aquarium department of a pet store or at hardware stores.

Acid Rain, Go Away

Acid rain is a problem in many areas around the world. How does the soil that absorbs the rain water affect the pH of the water after it flows through it? This experiment will test the pH of the water after it flows through the soil to see if it's still acidic.

PROBLEM/PURPOSE

Which types of soils can best neutralize acid rain?

EXPERIMENT SUMMARY

Using different types of soil, you'll pour acid water through them and then test the pH of the filtered water.

WHAT YOU NEED

▶ **Spade for digging**
▶ **6 plastic plant containers, 1 quart (.95 L) each**
▶ **6 plastic bowls**
▶ **Tape**
▶ **Marker**
▶ **Measuring cup**
▶ **1½ gallons (5.7 L) vinegar**
▶ **1½ gallons (5.7 L) tap water**
▶ **Plastic gallon (3.8 L) milk jug (thoroughly rinsed)**
▶ **pH paper (wide range)***

Can be purchased from a science supply catalog or borrowed from your science teacher

EXPERIMENTAL PROCEDURE

1. Using the spade, obtain soil samples from three different locations. Choose locations with different types of soil (for example, one that looks like clay, one mostly sand, one mixed, etc.)

2. Number the pots and plastic bowls 1 through 6.

3. Fill pots 1 and 2 with one of the soil samples. Fill the pots all the way up to the first lip of the pot so there's the same amount in each. Pack down the soil as you fill the pots to eliminate air pockets.

4. Repeat step 3 filling pots 3 and 4 with soil sample 2.

5. Repeat step 3 filling pots 5 and 6 with soil sample 3.

6. Mix 4 cups (.96 L) of vinegar and 4 cups (.96 L) of water into the milk jug. Shake the solution in the jug until it's thoroughly mixed.

7. Measure and record the pH of the vinegar solution.

8. Place the corresponding bowl under pot 1.

9. Holding pot 1 above the bowl, pour the solution onto the soil sample 1. Be sure to pour the whole solution and get all areas of the soil wet. Hold the pot above the bowl until all of the solution has dripped through. Set it aside.

10. Repeat steps 6 through 9, except use pots 3 and 5 and their corresponding bowls to catch the liquid.

11. Thoroughly rinse the milk jug, and then fill it with 2 quarts (1.9 L) of tap water.

12. Measure and record the pH of the tap water.

13. Using pot 2 and bowl 2, pour the water through the soil as you did in step 9. Hold the pot above the soil until all the water has dripped through. Set it aside.

14. Repeat step 13 using pots 4 and 6 and their corresponding bowls.

15. Measure and record the pH of the remaining liquids in bowls 1 through 6.

CONCLUSION

Look at the pH measurements before and after the experiment. Did any of the soil samples change the pH of the water? What about the vinegar solution? Which soil sample best neutralized (closest to pH 7) the vinegar solution? Can you recommend which type of soil neutralizes acids best? A note for evaluating your results: A change of 1 on

The effects of acid rain on a once-forested mountain top

the pH scale represents a tenfold increase. For example, a solution with a pH of 4 is ten times more acidic than a solution with a pH of 5 and 100 times more acidic than a solution with a pH of 6!

TAKE A CLOSER LOOK

● Acid rain can exist as other forms—snow, sleet, hail, fog, or anything that involves water. The acid found in it can be fairly strong. One acid produced in our atmosphere is carbonic acid—the same acid that's in soda. It's simply produced by water mixing with carbon dioxide (the stuff we exhale). So, even non-polluted rainwater is slightly acidic (pH of 5 to 6). Carbonic acid is somewhat weak, but in excess amounts it can also do some damage to plants and react with limestone to corrode away historical statues. Other gases that lead to acid rain are sulfur dioxide and nitrogen oxides. These also react with water to produce some pretty strong acids—sulfuric acid and nitric acid.

● The acetic acid (vinegar) used in this experiment is obviously not falling from our skies; however, it's a good substitute for a strong acid, such as the ones mentioned above.

● Acid rain may leach important elements from the soil. Some of these elements, such as aluminum, can damage cells in the water-transporting tubes of trees, causing them to literally die of thirst! It may also harm or kill soil bacteria and fungi, which are important to plant growth.

● Some soil types are more sensitive to acids due to the minerals contained in the soil and the thickness of the topsoil.

WHAT ELSE YOU CAN DO

● Get a soil test kit from your science teacher or a science supply catalog, and test the soil samples to see what types of minerals they contain. Also, use different types of acids to run the test (ask your science teacher to recommend some.)

● Repeat the experiment using soils from different parts of the country—a coastal region, a mountainous region, near a river, in the desert.

● Spray plants with different vinegar/water solutions (varying the percentage of vinegar for each plant tested) to see how much acid plants can handle before growth is affected.

DISPLAY TIPS

● Display your soil samples and used pH paper on the table for the judges to see. Include acid rain facts on your display board.

Rust Busters

If you've ever been to the beach, you probably know that you have to wash your chairs and bicycle with fresh water to get the salt off and prevent rusting. What if you could design a bicycle for the beach with the metal of your choice: one that would produce the least amount of rust? Based on your observations of metals in items you see daily, which type would you think is most rust-resistant?

PROBLEM/PURPOSE

Which metal is most rust-resistant?

EXPERIMENT SUMMARY

In this 10-day experiment, you'll cut pieces of different metals and submerge them in tap water and saltwater to see which is most rust-resistant.

WHAT YOU NEED

- ▶ **Measuring cup**
- ▶ **Spoon**
- ▶ **10 clear cups or test tubes**
- ▶ **Tap water**
- ▶ **Salt**
- ▶ **Masking tape**
- ▶ **Marker**
- ▶ **10 pencils**
- ▶ **12 inches (30.5 cm) of silver wire cut in half**
- ▶ **12 inches (30.5 cm) of steel wire cut in half**
- ▶ **12 inches (30.5 cm) of zinc wire cut in half**
- ▶ **12 inches (30.5 cm) of copper wire cut in half**
- ▶ **12 inches (30.5 cm) of aluminum wire cut in half**

EXPERIMENTAL PROCEDURE

1. Mix 1 tablespoon (14 g) of salt into 1 cup (.24 L) of water with a spoon. Stir until all salt crystals dissolve.

2. Label cups or test tubes as follows:

Cup 1: water + silver

Cup 6: saltwater + silver

Cup 2: water + steel

Cup 7: saltwater+ steel

Cup 3: water + zinc

Cup 8: saltwater + zinc

Cup 4: water + copper

Cup 9: saltwater + copper

Cup 5: water + aluminum

Cup 10: saltwater + aluminum

3. Organize your cups on a long table where you can leave them for 10 days. Place them in a row so that you can easily view them over the course of the experiment.

4. Wrap one end of each piece of wire around the middle of the pencil

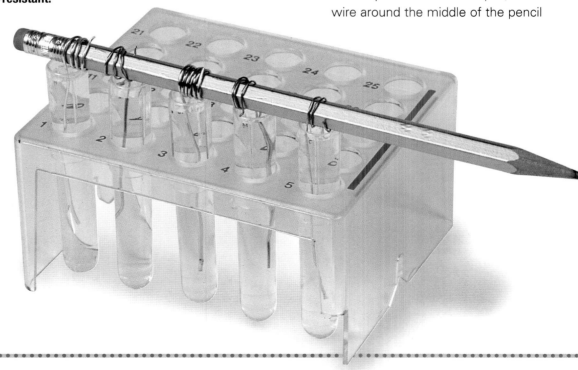

so that the end hangs down to the bottom of the cup. The pencil should be able to rest on the top of the cup with the wire suspended into the cup and touching the bottom. You may have to try several times to get the placement just right. Be sure to keep the wires and cups organized to avoid mistakes and mix-ups!

5. Pour tap water into the cups that require tap water until the cup is full.

6. Pour the saltwater solution into the cups that require saltwater until the cups are full.

7. Check your cups daily for 10 days. Note any changes in the metals in your notebook.

CONCLUSION

Were there any changes in the metals in tap water versus saltwater? If so, which metals produced more rust in the saltwater? Did any produce just as much in the tap water as the saltwater? Did the metals rust evenly along the wire? Or were some rusting more at the bottom or top? If so, why? Based on your data, which metal would you recommend for bikes or beach chairs?

TAKE A CLOSER LOOK

● Rusting is the result of a process called *oxidation*. Just like the word sounds, it involves oxygen in the air or water. Metals containing iron react with oxygen to produce *iron oxide*—this is the orange/brown color you see. When the rust flakes off, more metal is exposed to oxygen and the oxidation process continues corroding. Other metals can oxidize, such as aluminum and copper. Aluminum reacts with oxygen to form *aluminum oxide*. Although it may not look nice, this product actually protects the aluminum underneath from further corrosion. Copper corrodes by producing *copper carbonate*—the green color you may have noticed on objects, such as the Statue of Liberty.

WHAT ELSE YOU CAN DO

● Perform the same experiment using the recommended metal from your findings, except change the percentage of salt added to the tap water in each cup. For example, test the metal in a 5-percent salt solution, 25-percent, 50-percent, etc., to see if it rusts.

● Obtain a sample of ocean water or research the salinity of ocean water and make it yourself. Then, perform the test using this solution.

DISPLAY TIPS

● Display your metal wires on your display board with samples that haven't been tested, to show corrosion and rusting.

More advice from another real, live science teacher:

● Ask for a science fair school lab after school to help you and your classmates work on your projects.

● Organize a group of parent volunteers to dedicate time after school for advice and help. Or if you're close to a university, ask your science teacher if he or she can pair you and your classmates with college science students to form a mentoring program.

● Attractiveness of the display is a major step in selling your project to the judges. Look at your project as a t.v. commercial: you want to catch the judges attention and HOLD IT.

● You can actually take a previous science fair project and expand on it by doing more experiments. Remember, quantity of data quantifies the results.

● Tried and True results in blue (ribbon, of course!).

—Preston House,
6th-grade science teacher

Acid Battle

Your stomach is full of very strong acids—strong enough to burn a hole through a wooden desk. Thankfully, your stomach also produces a *bicarbonate*, or a basic solution, that keeps the acid from eating through your stomach. However, sometimes the acid overwhelms your stomach and ugh! You've got acid indigestion.

PROBLEM/PURPOSE

Which type of antacid can best neutralize stomach acid?

EXPERIMENT SUMMARY

You'll test some household products against name brand antacids to see which work best at neutralizing hydrochloric acid.

WHAT YOU NEED

- ▶ Latex gloves
- ▶ Safety goggles
- ▶ Apron
- ▶ 5 boiled eggs
- ▶ Mortar and pestle (borrowed from your science teacher)
- ▶ Kitchen scales, or scales from your science teacher
- ▶ 2 different name-brand antacid tablets
- ▶ 1 bottle name-brand liquid antacid
- ▶ 1 paper cup
- ▶ Baking soda

- ▶ 6 glass beakers (50 or 100 mL)
- ▶ Tape
- ▶ Marker
- ▶ Muriatic acid (dilute solution of hydrochloric acid)*
- ▶ pH paper (wide range)**
- ▶ 6 glass stirring rods (borrowed from your science teacher)

*Can be found at hardware stores—used for cleaning masonry and maintaining swimming pools

**Can be purchased through a science supply company or supplied by your science teacher

EXPERIMENTAL PROCEDURE

1. (Before you begin the experiment, get approval from the science fair coordinator to use muriatic acid.) make sure you're in a well-ventilated area. The fumes from the acid can be quite strong! Also, wear a long-sleeved shirt, long pants, and close-toed shoes. Put on your latex gloves, safety goggles, and apron. This is to protect your eyes, skin, and clothes from the acid

you'll be working with, in case it splashes. Finally, make sure you have an adult assist you by handling the acid throughout this experiment.

2. Remove the eggshells from the boiled eggs after they cool, and put them in the mortar. Grind the shells with the pestle until you get a fine powder. Set them aside.

3. Using the kitchen scales, determine the mass of two tablets from one of the name brands you chose. Write the mass down so you won't forget it. Use this mass as your standard for measuring the mass of the other materials. Set the tablets aside.

4. Measure the second name-brand tablets so that the mass is equal to

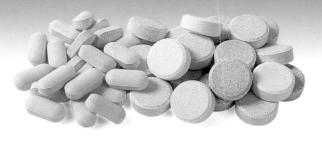

the standard. You may have to cut the tablets or grind them up and use pieces to get an equivalent mass. Set the tablets aside.

5. Determine the mass of the small paper cup. Pour the liquid antacid into it until it equals the mass of the standard plus the mass of the cup. Set it aside.

6. Measure the baking soda so that the mass is equal to the standard. Set it aside.

7. Measure the eggshells so that the mass is equal to the standard. Set them aside.

8. Label beakers 1 through 6 with tape and a marker.

9. Into each beaker, carefully pour 1 ounce (30 mL) of muriatic acid.

10. Using the pH paper, measure and record the pH of the muriatic acid.

11. In beaker 2, add the tablets from step 3.

12. In beaker 3, add the second name-brand tablets from step 4.

13. In beaker 4, add the liquid antacid from step 5.

14. In beaker 5, add the baking soda from step 6.

15. In beaker 6, add the eggshells from step 7.

16. Stir each beaker using a different stirring rod, until the reaction (if any) stops.

17. Using the pH paper, measure and record the pH of each solution.

CONCLUSION

Was there any difference in the pH of the muriatic acid and the final solutions? Which beakers produced the greatest increase in pH? Did any beakers stay the same? If the pH reached 7, neutralization occurred. Based on this information, which type of material would you suggest someone use for an antacid? Research the materials used in the name-brand antacids you chose. Are any the same as baking soda or eggshells? Use a bar graph to display your before and after results. Perform the test again to get more valid results.

TAKE A CLOSER LOOK

● Muriatic acid is a dilute solution of hydrochloric acid. It's commonly used to maintain the pH of pool water and clean masonry. Hydrochloric acid is the very strong acid found in your stomach (the stuff that can burn holes through desks!). So, why is it in our stomachs? The acid actually helps us digest food—without it we would have a hard time digesting meats and some vegetables. Our stomachs are protected by cells in an inner layer that secrete a bicarbonate-rich solution. This solution neutralizes the acid and produces water in the process. Indigestion occurs when the acid level in the stomach is too high. In some people, due to poor blood supply in the stomach or overproduction of acid, the bicarbonate secretion doesn't work as well—that's what causes ulcers. Ulcers are actually areas in the stomach that have been eaten away by the acid. They do heal, and medications can be taken to speed up this process.

WHAT ELSE YOU CAN DO

● Test the pH of various household solutions to determine which ones are acids and bases.

Ice Breakers

Whenever a snowstorm hits a city or town, it's only a matter of time before the trucks are out clearing the roads and spreading road salt to melt the snow and ice. Unfortunately, all that extra salt can cause damage to soil and lakes.

PROBLEM/PURPOSE

What is a good alternative to road salt for melting ice on sidewalks and roads?

EXPERIMENT SUMMARY

You'll use dishes of ice as your sidewalks and roads, and spread different materials sometimes used to melt ice. You'll then compare their ice-melting abilities to that of the road salts.

WHAT YOU NEED

- ► **6 casserole dishes, 9 x 13 inches (22.9 x 33 cm)**
- ► **Water**
- ► **Use of a freezer**
- ► **12 ounces (336 g) each of road salt, calcium chloride, fertilizer, sand, and cat litter**
- ► **Stopwatch**

EXPERIMENTAL PROCEDURE

1. Fill each dish with 1 inch (2.5 cm) of water.

2. Put each dish in the freezer until the water is completely frozen. If your freezer isn't big enough, you can experiment with one dish at a time.

3. Remove the dishes from the freezer and place each one in the same room on a table or floor.

4. Spread 12 ounces (336 g) of road salt, calcium chloride, fertilizer, sand, and cat litter evenly onto each of the ice dishes, one ingredient per dish. Spread the material evenly, and try not to clump the material in one spot. Leave one dish with no material on it at all as your control.

5. Observe the melting rates of the ice in each of the dishes. Record the time it took each dish to melt completely.

CONCLUSION

Compare the melting rates of the five dishes compared to the road salt dish. Did any come close to the time it took the salted ice to melt? After analyzing your results, do you feel any of the other materials could become a good replacement for road salt? Compare melting rates, price, and availability to reach a conclusion.

TAKE A CLOSER LOOK

● Most cities find that the cheapest and most effective way to melt snow and ice on pavement is to use road salt, also known as *sodium chloride*, which melts the snow

and ice by lowering the temperature at which freezing can occur. Sounds great, but many cities have to use hundreds of thousands of tons of the stuff to keep their roads clear. That much salt could end up in the drinking water, and too much salt could cause health problems, including high blood pressure. Road salt can also be harmful to lakes and streams. Think about it—it's like shaking salt into a freshwater aquarium.

WHAT ELSE YOU CAN DO

● If you found a good alternative to road salt, set up an experiment in which you test that material's effects on the environment. Water several potted plants with water solutions containing different amounts of the ingredient. Compare and record the plants' growths.

● Research how salt affects plant growth, and devise an experiment in which some plants are fed a salt-water solution and others are fed freshwater.

DISPLAY TIPS

● Bring in samples of the materials used in the experiment, and create icicle-like letters for your display title.

Acknowledgments

Many of the projects in this book were inspired by real science fairs projects. We'd like to thank the following students for their hard work on the topics and projects they worked on:

Holly Aldridge: Where There's Secondhand Smoke...
Carl Allison: The Sound of Music
Jessica Anderson: Acid Battle
Jonathan Angeles: The Sound of Music
Rob Benepe: Paper or Plastic
Sara Bernardi: Get a Grip
Lara Beth Poteat: Bacteria Wars
Ryan Cecil: Paper or Plastic
Sara Cefalu: Bubblerama!
Will Chambers: Paper or Plastic
Erin Cowan: Meteorologists Take Shelter!
Emilie Crigler: The Nose Knows
Carley Dameron: Ah...Refreshing!
David Dempsey: Acid Rain, Go Away
Judson Eley: Acid Rain, Go Away
Miriam George: Acid Battle
Julie Goodstadt: Memories
Julie Claire Guest: The Chilling Facts
Lisa Harris: What's That Smell? Oh, It's Me!
Katherine Horine: Family Fingerprints
Mattie Horine: Ice Breakers
Corbin Jennings: Paper or Plastic
Koeun Lee: The Grass is Greener
Olivia McCarrick: Caffeinated Typing
Mary McCoy: Color Confusion
Jessie Nix: Time for Your Veggies
Emma Norton: Ah...Refreshing!
Irene Palmer: Acid Rain, Go Away
Christiane Pheil: Under Pressure
Jarret Porter: Chromatography: What's in a Color?
Drew Reitz: Acid Rain, Go Away
Lauren Richardson: The Grass is Greener
Dillon Roop: Where There's Secondhand Smoke...
Jordan Scruggs: Pointing North
William Selle: The Balance of Nature
Edward Selle: The Balance of Nature
Zack Silver: The Power of Electromagnets
Parteek Singla: Food for the Beans
Kristi Stricker: Where There's Secondhand Smoke...
Molly Sweetser: Bubblerama!
Penn Tarleton: The Sound of Music
Cece Thomas: Pointing North

Allison Trask: Dueling Densities!

We'd also like to thank the following students for submitting their projects for consideration: **Will Albrecht, Christopher Baker, Danny Balck, Norah Bate, Ben Burt, Eric Christianson, Eric Dischinger, Hannah Fritschner, Alex Gershon, Sarah Gillespie, Michael Gore, David Grinstaff, Anna Klein, Carolyn Kubitschek, Spencer Legget, Kyler McClure, Julie Ann Olbrantz, Todd Olsen, Catie Pike,** and **Scott Russell**.

Our models also deserve special attention, especially since they really got into the spirit of this book, and had a lot of fun doing it: **Katherine Horine, Mattie Horine, Julie Claire Guest, Sara Cefalu, Penn Tarleton, Chris McDevitt, Johnny Grimes Lloyd, Clayton Armstrong, Lauren Richardson, Koeun Lee, Reed Cluxton, Eric Edgerton, Sebastian Barrett,** and **Alexandra Fisher**.

One great, big thank you goes to **Hope Pendergrass**. She's a wonderful teacher and a good friend who went above and beyond the call of duty to make sure we had a good book.

We'd like to extend a special thank you to **Mark Levin** and the folks at Carolina Day School (Asheville, NC) for all their assistance. They were essential to this project from the very beginning. Thanks also go out to **Dora Nelson, Howard Yarlborough, Andy Lammers,** and **Molly Lammers.**

Others to whom we are indebted:
Jennifer Camill of Hendersonville Middle School (Hendersonville, NC), for all of her help and enthusiasm
Beth Granato of Asheville Middle School (Asheville, NC) and **Jane Barkley** of Waynesville Middle School (Waynesville, NC), for corralling student projects for us to pour through
Roper Cleland, intern extraordinaire and

Index

author of "What's Really in the Food You're Eating?" (page 27)

Rain Newcomb, for diving in headfirst and helping us with the photography

Evan Bracken and **Richard Hasselberg**, for capturing the look of this book with their photographs

R. Anson Eaglin (USDA), **Carla Wallace** (NOAA), and **Steve Wilke** (Bergey Windpower Co, Inc), for their help locating wonderful photos

Malcolm Loughlin and **Ernest Biddy**, for giving us access to their science fairs

Charlie Pierce and **Shelly Mehlen**, for lending their hands, humor, and fruit to our experiments

Dr. Brian Gualano, for use of his dynamometer

And finally, the extraordinary cast of characters at Lark Books, including Dawn Cusick, Deborah Morgenthal, Carol Taylor, Rob Pulleyn, Thom Gaines, Theresa Gwynn, Kathy Holmes, Todd Kaderabek, Rosemary Kast, and Jeff Hamilton

Photography Credits

The photos on pages 87, 119, and 121 appear courtesy of Heather Smith.

The photos on pages 14, 52, and 57 (bacteria), appear courtesy of U.S. Department of Agriculture.

The photos on pages 21 and 35 appear courtesy of the Library of Congress.

The photos on pages 71, 73, 78, and 91 appear courtesy of the National Oceanic and Atmospheric Administration.

The photos on pages 38 and 65 (astronaut and asteroid), appear courtesy of NASA.

The wind turbine on page 102 appears courtesy of Bergey Windpower.

Corbis: Crop Duster (page 31), Bacteria Cultures (page 57), Dolphin in Tank (page 85), Traffic Jam on Freeway (page 92), Workers Cleaning Sidewalk (page 95), Tending to Crane Pulley (page 101)

West Stock: Girl Putting Vegetable Scraps into a Compost Pile (page 63) and Traffic in Winter (page 126)

Seattle Support Group: Hereford Cow and Red Beetle Bug (page 27) and House Rooftops (page 83)